A Pilgrim's History of the Rosary

Greg Firnstahl

WestBow
PRESS
A DIVISION OF THOMAS NELSON

Copyright © 2011 Greg Firnstahl

All rights reserved. No part of this book may be used or reproduced by any means, graphic, electronic, or mechanical, including photocopying, recording, taping or by any information storage retrieval system without the written permission of the publisher except in the case of brief quotations embodied in critical articles and reviews.

WestBow Press books may be ordered through booksellers or by contacting:

WestBow Press
A Division of Thomas Nelson
1663 Liberty Drive
Bloomington, IN 47403
www.westbowpress.com
1-(866) 928-1240

Because of the dynamic nature of the Internet, any web addresses or links contained in this book may have changed since publication and may no longer be valid. The views expressed in this work are solely those of the author and do not necessarily reflect the views of the publisher, and the publisher hereby disclaims any responsibility for them.

Any people depicted in stock imagery provided by Thinkstock are models, and such images are being used for illustrative purposes only.

Certain stock imagery © Thinkstock.

ISBN: 978-1-4497-2456-6 (sc)
ISBN: 978-1-4497-2454-2 (ebk)

Library of Congress Control Number: 2011914742

Printed in the United States of America

WestBow Press rev. date: 08/31/2011

Contents

Forward vii
Introduction ix

A Pilgrims History of the Rosary 1
    The Pagan's Search for Meaning 3
    Paganism 3
    Ireland's Pagan Neolithic Age And Spiritual Sources 4
    Ireland's Celtic Age 6

The Roots Of The Rosary In The Ancient Middle East 8
    Christianity's Messianic Spirituality 9
    Christ's Messianic Spirituality Spreads Beyond Israel's Shores ... 11

Ireland's Pre-Patrician Christianity 14
    Repetitive Prayer Evolves Around the Mediterranean 15
    Repetitive Prayer During St. Patrick's Time 16

Council of Ephesus 431 24

Prayer Gains Momentum 25
    The Clergy Reaches Out to the Laity 28
    "Teach Us to Pray"
    The Na Tri Coicat Format is Introduced to the Laity 28
    A New Repetitive Prayer Form Is Introduced 29

The Psalters 31
    The Psalter of 150 Our Fathers 31
    The Psalter of 150 Hail Marys 31
    The Hail Mary Is Published 31

The Albigensian Heresy 33
    The Albigensian Heretics 33
    Dominic's Life and the Albigensian Heretics 33

The Hail Mary is Joined to the Our Father 37

The Psalters (Continued) 38
   The Psalter of 150 Affirmations of Faith in Christ,
   The Jesus Psalter 38
   150 Praises of the Blessed Virgin 39
   Henry of Kalkar 41
   Dominic the Prussian 41
   The Psalter of the Rosary's 15 Mysteries and The
   Psalter of the Rosary's 15 Tablets 42

Personalities and Doctrine 43
   Alan de Rupe Shapes the Rosary's Structure 43
   Pope Pius V 44
   Pope Pius V and the Battle of Lepanto 46
   Endorsements Follow 48
   Albert di Castello 49
   Jansenism Heresy and St. DeMontfort 49
   DeMontfort and the Jansenists 49
   Assumption of the Blessed Virgin Mary 50
   The Luminous Mysteries 52

Introducing the Rosary Concept 55
   The Joyful Mysteries 58
   The Luminous Mysteries 58
   The Sorrowful Mysteries 59
   The Glorious Mysteries 59

Praying the Rosary 61

Reflections on the Mysteries of The Rosary 65
   The Joyful Mysteries 67
   The Luminous Mysteries 70
   The Sorrowful Mysteries 73
   The Glorious Mysteries 75

Final Thoughts 79

Recommwding List 81

Forward

My dear friends, over the years I have given prayer to this writing. I would like to say that I have reached spiritual heights, but I have not. I would like to claim a perfect Christian life, but I am still growing. I want to say I pray the Rosary perfectly and have achieved a deep union with God, but I am still maturing. However, I have learned to walk with God and continually ask him to "keep working with me" (Mk. 16:20). For me, the Rosary has made me a better Christian, more Christ-like, a little more understanding about life and people. I look at this writing the same way the little child in the Scriptures looked at his five loaves and two fish he gave the Lord. It is a small offering (John 6:9ff).

Introduction

Praying and meditating on the Rosary's messianic Mysteries of Faith has taught me that nothing I go through in my life, as easy or hard as it seems at the time, can separate me from the love of God, and that union with Him awaits me in this life as it does for every Christian that places his or her faith in the saving power of Jesus Christ. Devotion to Our Lady teaches me how much it is a natural development to my Christian faith. It is nothing to shy away from or be embarrassed about. I should not feel awkward about developing it because it is the will of God and Jesus is so intimately united with Mary one cannot be separated from the other. She supports Christ's life, work, message and ministry. She is his mediator, while he is the mediator between heaven and earth. Therefore, devotion to Our Lady is rooted totally in Jesus and all that he is and means under heaven and earth. That is why I have such confidence in devotion to Our Lady. It is totally in union with Jesus' will.

Meditations on the Rosary's Mysteries of Faith unfold what Jesus and Mary mean to me personally. They unfold the ordinary lives of Jesus, Mary and Joseph for the first thirty years of our Lord's life. The last three years of His life were different and challenging for him and his mother. They faced moments filled with divine illumination and enjoyed life while they learned to manage their personal suffering one day at a time. The Resurrection changed peoples' view of Jesus, His message and ministry.

Learning how to pray the Rosary properly was a process of success and failure with this prayer. When I pray the Rosary properly, Mary intercedes for others and me. She " . . . intercedes for us before the Father who filled her with grace and before the Son born of her womb, praying with us and for us." If I fail to pray the Rosary properly then it becomes a "body without a soul, and its recitation runs the risk of becoming a mechanical repetition of formulas," in violation of Christ's admonition not to heap up words and empty phrases while we pray to God (Mt. 6: 7). Thus I am a success or failure by the way I pray the Rosary. As a failure, I will not reflect a strong Christian witness, and if I don't improve my prayer, I will slide into sin and not live in the state of grace. As a success, I will pray the Rosary properly and be in union with Mary and her prayers offered to Jesus on behalf of others and myself.

There is wisdom in praying the Rosary. It leads me to a wise contemplative experience in prayer. How important it is for me to settle down, focus on God in a quiet place and prepare myself to meditate on the Rosary's messianic Mysteries of Faith. Most importantly, I know how essential it is to remain silent after praying the Rosary, to take the opportunity to stay before the presence of God in peaceful solitude, allowing the grace of this prayer to penetrate more deeply into my soul. In my opinion, this is the most important part of praying the Rosary: remain still. Let God unfold His Presence: "Be still and know that I am God" (Ps. 46:10).

I serve as a witness to the Rosary and I ask you to journey with me. Embark with me along this great spiritual path. As John Paul II wrote in his Apostolic Letter, *On the Most Holy Rosary*, *Rosarium Virginis Mariae*, "Today we are facing new challenges. Why should we not once more have recourse to the Rosary, with the same faith as those who have gone before us? You therefore are now invited to read it in a spirit of attentive good will . . . ." (See Sirach's Forward).

Learning about the Rosary takes us on a faith journey. We will start with its history, touch on its spiritual sources and some of its great advocates, battles, promulgations and blessings. All of it may be reduced to one simple statement: how much Jesus and Mary love us and to what extent they are willing to prove it.

After we have looked at the Rosary's history, we will be faced with a question: do you want to pray it? For those who want to go on and pray it, I have included a section for that purpose. By praying the Rosary we also learn to walk with God throughout the course of our daily lives. I believe this is what praying the Rosary is all about: walking with God throughout the course of our daily lives through all the joys, sorrows, and new beginnings life offers us.

A Pilgrims
History of the Rosary

The Pagan's Search for Meaning

The pagan's search for meaning was unending. It makes no difference what generation you refer to. They were trying to make some sense of their lives: all their divisions and strife, good and evil, ephemeral beauty, sensual and material pleasures. Life held few solutions for them and the best they could do, if they wanted a more meaningful life filled with hope, was to create and follow their own religious traditions, for example: make good human and animal sacrifices, gain more goods, grow better crops and herds. Abundance and self-fulfillment were their goals. This caused uneasiness in their hearts. There were no guarantees. An ultimate truth was evading them. It is this people God would reach out to and save through the Catholic Church (the Church), its sacramental and devotional life, specifically the Rosary. The Rosary would someday give these people hope, a hope they never had before for a more meaningful life.

Paganism

From an etymological standpoint, the word "paganism" comes from the Latin word *paganus,* meaning "a country dweller," someone living in the country. In practical terms pagans lived in both the city and the country. They had no boundaries. Their lives were lived day by day. Their religious system was polytheistic (belief in more than one god), self-centered, and self-gratifying. One truth was certain: pagans had a certain religious depravity about them that needed redeeming—to be brought from spiritual darkness into Christianity's spiritual light through the preaching of the gospel, the Church's sacramental life and its devotional prayer tradition, the Rosary.

It is at this point that we turn to Ireland's pagan age and expose ourselves to some of its religious elements so we can learn something about those to whom the gospel and Rosary would someday be presented.

Ireland's Pagan Neolithic Age And Spiritual Sources

To begin with, our knowledge of pagan Ireland is quite limited. We can only hope to highlight some basic religious traditions important to its primitive culture. For the Irish, we know paganism was their way of life because of the religious festivals and customs they kept during both the Neolithic Age and the Celtic Age. It would remain this way for millennia to come before Christianity would slowly emerge on the Irish scene with its saving sacramental life and gospel message. Once these sacred traditions were rooted in this primitive culture then the Rosary as a devotional prayer would begin to slowly emerge.

As early as Ireland's Neolithic Age, 3000 B.C.-500 B.C, the pagans had one objective in mind: to survive. There was little time for philosophical speculation. They had to do whatever it took to live. It meant they had to rely on their natural instincts. Every day on the eastern side of Ireland in the county Meath area, these pagans started out with the same objective in mind: to sustain self and family. For example, this might lead them to a stream or a lake to fish; or to a forest or meadow to hunt game; or to fetch water; or pick fruits; chop wood; or cut down a tree to build a shelter. At the end of the day these people would sleep well if they succeeded in acquiring enough to live on; or they might not sleep so soundly if they had not done so well, wondering if their days were numbered. Life hung in the balance.

To help these Irish pagans succeed they turned to religion as a way of spiritually connecting with the physical world of lakes, water wells, forest groves and hills as examples. This type of religious connection to nature gave them meaning for the harsh reality they faced day after day. It helped them develop a confidence that they could communicate with the spirit world and thus gain its blessing to help them survive. So we shall see that the Irish on the eastern side of Ireland communicated with the spirits by creating mythologies, gods (like the sun god Lugh or Balor) goddesses (like Anu Brigitte, Beltine and Danu) and religious festivals, such as the Solstices' and Equinoxes' for example. These traditions helped them express themselves. Some of the special places where these traditions were celebrated were Newgrange (Si an Bru), a prehistoric monument located in County Meath on the eastern side of Ireland, and the Ceide Fields, (Achaid Cheide, meaning "field of the flat—topped hill") where the

Summer Solstice, Autumn Equinox, Winter Solstice, and Spring Equinox were celebrated.

The Spring Equinox, (Equinox means "equal night") was celebrated March twenty-first and sacrifices were offered to Anu, the Celtic goddess of plenty and Mother Earth, because the earth was considered sacred by the Irish. This celebration marked the occasion when the sun gave its power to the earth to grow fruits from the community's seven sacred trees (oak, hazel, apple, yew, ash, holly and pine); the most important were the hazel and apple.

The next celebration was the Summer solstice, an astronomical term referring to the position of the Sun in relation to the celestial equator which includes one longest day and shortest night. On June twenty-first this celebration takes place. It honors the sun's power at its greatest intensity. Sacrifices are offered to the sun god Lugh, gathered and later on burned in an oak fire. Coals are spread over fields to make them fertile for the coming year.

The Autumn Equinox was celebrated on September twenty-first. This celebration focused on the Corn King (a real person) who offered his life for the community. His remains were placed under a Cromlech, a monolith encircling a mound. Each year the community gathered at the Corn King's burial site and placed rocks there, memorializing the sacrifice he made for his community's future well-being.

The last festival was the Winter Solstice, celebrated on December twenty-first; it marked the day of the "new sun" while the old one faded off into the distance. This symbolized the actions of two birds: a wren, a small brownish songbird, having rounded wings, a slender bill, and a short, often erect tail; and a robin. The robin killed the wren. This meant the beginning of new life.

These religious celebrations marked important times in Ireland's Neolithic pagan culture. They helped the people communicate with their gods and goddesses to hopefully earn their continued blessings. However, these people knew they were vulnerable to life and death so they had little choice but to place their faith and confidence in these celebrations in order to gain the support of their gods. Centuries would pass before Ireland's next age would emerge, the Celtic Age (500 B.C.-400A.D.).

Ireland's Celtic Age

From 500 B.C. Ireland's pagans were known as Celts. The Celts introduced a more sophisticated spirituality that did not coincide with the solstices and equinoxes of farmers. These people were cattlemen. Their festivals were Imbolc (Imbolg), Beltine, Lughnasa (Lunasa) and Samhain (Samain).

The Imbolc (Candlemas) festival was celebrated February first. The bright sun began to emerge. The death of winter was finished. A boar was sacrificed. The goddess Brigitte (goddess of Darkness) sent three rays of light to unfreeze the ground, to unfreeze the water and to establish fire. Brideogs, women dressed in white, danced in the fields to follow the path of the sun.

The Beltine, goddess of the Soul, festival was held on May first. On the eve the chief Druid (Chief Cleric or Spiritual Master) would light a fire on the hill of Uisneagh, a place where provincial kings would meet. Other druids, a sub-class of cleric, would light fires from the central fire so that the rest of Ireland could then draw from their fires. The sun god Lugh danced and the festivities began. Couples leaped through fire to give them fertility while farmers drove their cattle between fires to expel evil spirits from them.

The festival of Lughnasa, the main god of Celtic mythology, was celebrated on the first of August and featured three parts—religious, commercial and social—lasting nine days. The sun god, Lugh, meaning "light" or "shining", was an ancient pagan god from the Tuatha De Danann ("People of the goddess Danu") tribe, a divine Irish race whose name is now encompassed in the Irish for word for August. During Lughnasa, a sacrifice was offered each evening for nine days on *Cruachan Aigli*, known as Croagh Patrick (Patrick's Mountain). Since it was a social event, sports were played, including chariot racing and hurling. Food was brought and made into a sacrificial offering decorated with stones.

The last festival was Samhain ("Summer's End"), celebrated on November first. Farmers drove their cattle over cliffs to kill them and burn their bones in bonfires to release their spirits back into the air. The gates of our earth were rolled back. Spirits roamed the earth. People wore masks to protect themselves. Fear dominated. As the celebration ended, a "new sun" brightly shone forth. Hope was restored. New life began.

These primitive festivals marked a passage in Celtic history celebrated by the farmers of Newgrange and the Ceide Fields. These festivals nurtured the pagans' primitive faith, while at the same time it gave them the needed confidence to survive for another year. These festivals tell us how deeply dependant on nature the Irish pagans were; that all natural things were subject to supernatural influence; and that these pagans reflected a sense of fear and reverence toward creation. These people possessed an uncomplicated faith tradition in the spiritual world that would eventually embrace Christianity, especially the Rosary's way, truth, and life because its spirituality was so simple to practice, so profound it changed lives for the better, so salvific it saved souls for Christ and His mother Mary.

This primitive pagan spirituality would be replaced by the Church's gospel message, sacramental life and devotional spirituality, the Rosary. But first, spiritual groundwork needed to be done. Paganism still had its strongholds in the Irish culture.

While Ireland was going through its cultural and religious growing pains, a *meditative spirituality* was making itself known in another location: the Ancient Middle East.

The Roots Of The Rosary In The Ancient Middle East

Far away from Ireland, on the opposite side of Europe, across the Mediterranean in the ancient Middle East, lived another pagan people from the regions of Mesopotamia, Assyria, Egypt and Canaan for example. These pagans had cultivated a spirituality rooted in meditation that could be traced to "the dawn of recorded history." They engaged in prayerfully placing themselves in the presence of a religious deity such as the Canaanite god Ba al, for example. They cultivated a state of meditation by Waiting, Seeking or Searching. Such meditation fulfilled their emotional and spiritual needs. In this state of meditation they hoped to connect with the Sought One by repeatedly calling on his or her name for a blessing or an answer to a petition. This ancient tradition of meditation was adopted by Jesus' followers and assimilated into their own prayer tradition, which helped them meditate on the life of Christ, his family, message, and ministry. The Virgin Mother serves as our example. She was known by the early Christian community to "ponder" our Lord's life and times and "[keep] all these things in her heart" (Lk. 2:19, 51). This type of meditation tradition would eventually become part of the Rosary meditation tradition.

Christianity's Messianic Spirituality

As we shall see, during the time of Christ (5 BC-30 AD), Jesus' followers, especially his Virgin Mother, meditated on His messianic spirituality— "The Spirit of the Lord is upon me, because he has anointed me to preach good news to the poor. He has sent me to proclaim release to the captives and recovering of sight to the blind, to set at liberty those who are oppressed, to proclaim the acceptable year of the Lord" (Lk. 4:18-19). In essence, God continues to reach out to all mankind through His son Christ Jesus, his words and actions. Our Lord introduced a simple devotional prayer upon which the first century church would build its faith:

> **The Our Father** (Mt. 6:9-13)
> Our Father in heaven
> Hallowed be your name,
> Your kingdom come,
> Your will be done
> On earth as it is in heaven.
> Give us today our daily bread,
> And forgive us the wrong we have
> Done
> As we forgive those who wrong us.
> Subject us not to the trial
> But deliver us from the evil one.
> Amen.

The Our Father would serve a double purpose. It would become part of the sacred liturgy of the Mass and it would become part of many private devotional prayer forms in the Church and especially the Rosary. Through these actions and words Christ makes his Father present among men. All people, not just the Irish, could place their lives, uncertainties, and fears in the Father's care knowing he would provide for them (Ps. 146). This took faith—"the substance of things hoped for, the evidence of things not seen" (Heb. 11:1). The uneasiness in their hearts would vanish over time and their religious traditions would slowly be replaced with the gospel message and the Church's sacramental life. In fact, devotional faith in the early church community would begin flourishing.

Greg Firnstahl

Those responsible for writing about Christ's life and times were four of his evangelists, Matthew, Mark, Luke and John. Each one's account is considered a canonical "gospel," a writing that describes Christ's life, death and resurrection into heaven (around 30). These gospels were written between the years 65 and 95. Luke's, the longest, is the one we feature here.

It has a Prologue (1:1-4), Jesus' Infancy Narrative (1:5-2:52), Preparation for Public Ministry (3:1-4:13), Ministry in Galilee (4:14-9:50), Journey to Jerusalem and His Travel Narrative (9:51-19:27). It includes Jesus' Teaching Ministry in Jerusalem (19:28-21:38), Passion (22:21-23:56), and Resurrection Narrative (24:1-53).

Since there were so many biblical passages making up Luke's gospel, the Church started focusing on certain texts for devotional inspiration: 1:30-32; 1:42-43; 2:6-7; 2: 34-35; 2:48; 23:46; 24:6; and 24: 51. Other texts include the Gospel of Matthew: 3:13-17; 5-7; 17: 1-8; 26:26-30; the Gospel of John: 2:1-13; 19: 17; and the Book of Acts: 2:1-4. These texts lay the spiritual foundation upon which the Rosary would be built (for the Assumption of Mary, see Pius X, "*Munificentissimus*,"; and for the Coronation of Mary, see Pius XII, "*Ad Caeli Reainam*").

Christ's Messianic Spirituality Spreads Beyond Israel's Shores

Within the first century, the early Christian Church tried to figure out how to apply Christ's messianic spirituality in daily life, something we all struggle with, I know I do.

In the Acts of the Apostles, people met in the upper room in Jerusalem to pray continuously (Acts 1:14). Praying continuously became a way of life. Others left for Egypt to live as hermits, who prayed alone, or as cenobites, who prayed together in community. Their goal was to practice continuous prayer. Still others formed communities outside Jerusalem while many set sail for destinations like Ephesus, Greece and Italy. Those not content with the status quos journeyed deeper into Europe, some traveling to the shores of England, Ireland, Scotland and Wales.

Church of the Annunciation, built over the site, tradition holds, where the Virgin Mary lived at the time she had been chosen to be the Mother of God (Lk. 1:26-38). It may be said, following the Annunciation the Lord is with her whom He has filled with His grace and blessed. The expected Savior of nations is to come forth clothed in our humanity and her flesh.

This Silver Star marks the place where Jesus was born. Shortly thereafter, Mary wrapped him in swaddling clothes and laid him in a manger. Henceforth she leads a life in perpetual union with her son Jesus, sharing with Him His joys and sorrows (Lk: 2:1-7).

Here marks the place where Mary laid the infant Jesus in a manger. It is located less than 20 feet from the nativity, the place or location, where Jesus was born. How willingly will she hasten to our aid when we need her; with what love will she refresh us, and with what strength sustain us.

The Garden of Olives is situated on the Mount of Olives. Here in the Garden is where Christ's Passion began (Mk 14:32-35).
Some of these trees date back to that time.
"Let us go, that we may Die with him" (Jn. 11:16).

Here in the Upper Room is the place where Christ's followers Gathered for the descent of the Holy Spirit (Acts 2:1-11).

Greg Firnstahl

Ireland's Pre-Patrician Christianity

Christ's gospel message was reaching Ireland prior to the coming of St. Patrick (AD 387—March 17th, AD 493). Those who ventured onto Ireland's ancient shores probably came from England, bringing with them this same gospel, which confronted the Celt's pagan gods and religious practices they had been celebrating for the past several centuries before the time of Christ. These courageous Christians were few in number but strong in witness and their effects were lasting. We don't know all their names, but we know they evangelized the Celts who became Christians and some were ultimately canonized saints preceding the mission of Patrick; notably Ciaran of Saiger, Declan of Ardmore, Ibar of Beccere, Ailbe of Emly, M'eltioc of Kinsale, Mo-chanoc and Mo-chatoc. These were some of the brave saints that introduced Christianity to Ireland. What emerged was Celtic Christianity, a mixture of pagan practices and Christian spirituality.

When Patrick arrived in Ireland he was around forty six years old (AD 433). He had to deal with pagan Celts and Celtic Christians, not an easy task. Fortunately for him, predecessors like St Abben (AD 165), St Gunifort of Pavia, St Manusuetus of Toul (died AD 375) and Grimona of Soiussons had done their job, "The groundwork had been done and the foundations had been laid for a Celtic Church in Ireland that over the next few centuries would become one of the most vibrant parts of the Body of Christ." Patrick stepped into this situation, a man of God who faithfully engaged in repetitive prayer.

Repetitive Prayer Evolves Around the Mediterranean

Repetitive prayer began to evolve around the Mediterranean, not just in Ireland and different parts of Europe and the Middle East. By AD 360 monks, nuns and hermits had been counting their prayers using stones, cribbage boards and knotted cords. The rest of their prayer times were fixed, starting with morning prayer, followed by breakfast and mass in the community church. Midday prayer followed, then dinner, benediction, supper and night prayer. This schedule helped the religious fulfill their prayer obligation; they emphasized *quality, not quantity*, while providing an opportunity for scheduled readings. Fasting, certain penances, and memorizing from the Gospel of Mark was also done.

During the day the monks worked. While working they counted prayers by tossing stones. It was a never-ending cycle. When they finished praying they would start over again, gathering stones and putting them in a bag to be counted again. These stones were referred to as "prayer-counters." The hermit Paul of Egypt was famous for doing this (AD 360). He would fill his pocket with three hundred stones a day for praying. Others counted their prayers by walking around Holy Wells, a tradition I engaged in while in the village of Knock, in County Mayo on the west side of Ireland. Some terrain is rocky and uneven to walk around in parts but the effect of such a prayer was a calming one for me. After prayer there was a sense of accomplishment and a more intimate feeling of having drawn closer to Our Lord and Our Lady.

Greg Firnstahl

Repetitive Prayer During St. Patrick's Time

As Christianity established itself in Celtic Ireland, Catholic priests began blessing pagan wells, which are considered doorways to the spiritual world for the Irish, claiming them for sacramental purposes such as baptism, Mass and confirmation. Also, the faithful used them to count their prayers and meditate while walking around these special sacred sites. Patrick did the same thing. He also used holy wells to celebrate liturgies, evangelize people, baptize, ordain priests and bishops, and as a place of prayer (from AD 432-493 Patrick ministered as bishop in Ireland).

In AD 441 Patrick made his vigil on the summit of Croagh Patrick, Ireland's holy mountain, where legend has it he banished the snakes from Ireland. There Patrick counted prayers, lived and fasted for forty days and forty nights by imitating Christ's desert experience (Mt. 4:1-11). For the past 1500 years, pilgrims, including myself, have emulated St. Patrick by making this same trek up the summit to pray; counting prayers along the path; and drawing more closely to God in a cold, windy, wet environment.

Ballintubber Abbey, Claremorris, Co. Mayo, has been in use for the past 750 years, making it the oldest abbey in Ireland.

Ballintubber Abbey's Holy Well is reminiscent of what the Church used more than 750 years ago.

The Holy Well at Tobernalt in County Sligo is found in a primeval forest setting. The name "Tobernalt" means "well of the cliff." This well has an ancient past and a rich heritage. It is famous for hosting the feast of harvest known also as the Lughanasa festival celebrated on the first of August.
Six thousand years ago pagans considered this well a sacred place of worship. With the arrival of Christianity a fusion of traditions took place and it was consecrated by the church for its own use.

Water at Tobernalt's Holy Well is reputed to possess curative powers.

Tobernalt's Holy Altar is used today for Mass on special occasions.

In the foreground is "Mass Rock", where Saint Patrick offered the Divine Liturgy.

Mass Rock at Ballintubber Abbey.

Carrowneden Holy Well is famous for several reasons.

These words memorialize the occasion Saint Patrick offered Mass at the Well in 440 A.D.

According to the legend, while Saint Patrick was in prayer during the Liturgy, the stone he knelt on, shown here, molded to his knees. Can you find the imprints? Look closely.

The Path Leading up to Croagh Patrick

After awhile the climb becomes dangerous.

As the pilgrim nears the summit he has an opportunity to engage in penitential exercises, a tradition that started shortly after Saint Patrick's time when Our Fathers would have been among the first prayers said. Centuries would pass, perhaps as many as seven or eight, before the Church would approve the Hail Mary. At that time, it may have been incorporated into these penitential exercises. At Station One, Leacht Benain, named after Saint Patrick's disciple, Benignus, is a small circular cairn of stones the pilgrim walks around seven times saying seven Our Fathers, seven Hail Marys, and one Apostles' Creed.

Upon reaching the summit is Station Two. Here the pilgrim kneels and prays seven Our Fathers, seven Hail Marys and one Apostles' Creed.

After Station Two the pilgrim walks to the chapel and prays for the Pope's intentions, then circles it fifteen times clockwise praying fifteen Our Fathers, fifteen Hail Marys and one Apostles' Creed. In front of the chapel is Leaba Phadraig, Saint Patrick's bed, outlined with metal tubing. The pilgrim walks around the bed seven times saying seven Our Fathers and seven Hail Marys followed by an Apostles' Creed. On the other side of the mount, its westerly slope, not shown here, is Station Three, Roilig Mhuire, and the Virgin's Cemetery. Here sit three circular cairns. Believed to be a pre-Christian pagan burial site, the pilgrim circles each cairn seven times saying seven Our Fathers, seven Hail Marys and one Apostles' Creed. He then circles the whole site seven times repeating the same process.

Council of Ephesus 431

By AD 431 Christological questions regarding the person and work of Jesus Christ continued to surface and needed to be addressed by the Church, but not before a rigorous debate would take place. The forum would be held in Ephesus in the context of the Third Ecumenical Council where bishops from around the Mediterranean would meet to hear and decide the outcome of arguments.

The leading protagonist of this debate was Nestorius (AD 386-451), who taught that Mary was the mother of Jesus as a human being, but not the mother of God! Cyril of Alexandria (AD 376-444) presided over this council and became Nestorianism's chief opponent. Cyril argued that Nestorianism taught that the human and divine essences of Jesus were not one and the same person. That there are two essences, the man Jesus Christ and the divine Logos which dwelt in him. Thus Mary gave birth to only the human person Jesus, not the divine. So it was not possible for God to suffer or be crucified in the person Jesus. Nestorianism rejected these teachings. During this meeting, Cyril oversaw the condemnation of Nestorius' teaching. According to him, the people of Ephesus danced in the streets and paraded with torches in joy. As far as he was concerned, the matter was settled. Mary, the mother of Jesus, was officially recognized as *Theo-tokos,* Mother of God, and Jesus is both human and divine in one person, but two natures.

From a devotional standpoint this official recognition given to Mary by Ephesus' Third Ecumenical Council permitted the faithful to adore her through prayerful devotion. This meant devotion to Mary was now officially approved by the Church. People could pray to her because the Church had officially recognized her divine motherhood. The Church would build some of its fundamental spirituality on this truth about Mary the Mother of God as a great intercessor. The Rosary tradition would totally embrace this spirituality: Mary as Mother of God and intercessor for God's people. Praying with Mary was considered proper to do. "Hence the Church truly confesses that Mary is truly the 'Mother of God'" (*Theo-tokos*). *Catechism of the Catholic Church,* #495.

Prayer Gains Momentum

Around the end of the first millennium interest in repetitive prayer gained momentum. Catholics all over Europe wanted a devotional prayer for themselves like the religious enjoyed as they prayed the Divine Office (also known as *The Office*), which signifies a duty accomplished for God. Thus certain prayers are recited at fixed hours of the day or night by priests, religious or clerics, and in general, by all those obliged by their vocation to fulfill this duty.

The Church knew most of the laity lacked an education except for the wealthy who could afford it, but for the rest an education was out of the question. One of the main reasons was due to a lack of books. They were limited because the printing press had not been invented. Scribes had to write books by hand. Another problem was that all subjects were taught in Latin. To be educated meant one needed to learn how to read and master the Latin language. So how did the Church teach the uneducated to pray?

Just a few miles down Bulbul Mountain lays the ancient city of Ephesus, Turkey, the crossroads between Europe, Asia and the Middle East. Here ancient streets are still lined with white-columned ruins, some of the largest and best-preserved remnants of the once thriving Roman Empire.

Classic Ruins.

Down Nightingale Mountain at Ephesus, it is possible to see the very amphitheater described in Acts where the Ephesians' silversmiths rioted against St. Paul for teaching the Christian message (Acts 19; especially vv. 23-40). It is believed the theater held approximately twenty four thousand.

The Ephesus' Theater.

The main road leading to the Library of Celsus.

The Library of Celcus.

Greg Firnstahl

The Clergy Reaches Out to the Laity

A development evolved in the early church that helped the laity learn to pray. This development was the creation of Latin liturgical texts. These liturgical texts would become the precursor to the Psalters from which the Rosary would eventually evolve.

The Church developed these texts for the laity to celebrate daily liturgies by inserting short excerpts from the Church's official liturgical texts into a booklet form they could use during Mass. The text included sung parts such as the Kyrie; a short liturgical prayer that begins with the words "Lord, have mercy;" the Credo, or Creed; and the Sanctus, which is an ancient Christian hymn of adoration sung or said immediately before the prayer of consecration in the traditional liturgies. The laity memorized these prayers and considered the texts as prized possessions passing them down from generation to generation. Possessing one gave an edge not only for learning the liturgy but also for reciting prayers more effectively with the monks in choir.

"Teach Us to Pray"
The Na Tri Coicat Format is Introduced to the Laity

By AD 750 the Church was mentoring the laity in prayer. No stones were used. No Latin liturgical texts were crafted. The Church had to deal with the issue of praying the Divine *Office,* known also as the Liturgy of the Hours, which consists mostly of psalms supplemented by hymns and readings. At this time it was reserved solely for the religious to pray. The laity wanted to participate in this religious tradition normally said before or after the Liturgy.

A creative solution was proposed by a small group of Irish monks: the monks assigned to the laity a set of prayers to keep pace with them. Both groups would start together and finish together but use different prayers to achieve the same results.

To effect this change the monks used a long established prayer tradition known as the "*Na tri coicat*" format that divided the psalms into three groups of fifties. At Kemble and Canterbury, England, for example, the monks used this format to pray a set number of prayers for a benefactor or monk who had recently died.

St Patrick adapted this format for his own personal use by dividing his nighttime into three parts, devoting the first two parts to prayer and the last one to sleep. During part one he spent time praying the psalms, a group of fifty, making genuflections before and after each psalm. During part two he stood in cold water and extended his arm heavenward as he said his prayers in the context of performing penance.

In connection with the use of the "fifties" it is believed that the monks at St. Columba Abbey, Ireland, and the Abbey of St. Gall, Switzerland, brought this concept to the European continent. By the ninth century its usage had spread to parts of northern Italy and monasteries, including the Abbey of Reichenau, had adapted this tradition. These monasteries entered into an agreement to form a community of prayer. Each time a member of a monastic community died, mass was said along with "fifty" prayers.

Each group of fifty in the *"Na tri coicat"* format contained its own assigned meaning. Monks took this format and instructed the laity to pray Our Fathers in unison with them as they prayed the *Office*. In theory one Our Father equaled one psalm. Since the *Office* consisted of one hundred fifty Psalms, the monks substituted one hundred fifty Our Fathers for the laity to pray. In this way both groups kept pace with each other and the laity had the opportunity to pray its own version of the *Office*.

A New Repetitive Prayer Form Is Introduced

By AD 1115 this prayer custom was popularized and it had spread onto the European continent. The English embellished it by counting one hundred fifty Our Fathers (*Pater nosters*) on beads strung together by "Paternosterers". This was a slow evolving development of devotional prayer that took place throughout Ireland, England, Scotland and Wales plus other parts of the European continent. Repetitive prayer continued to slowly evolve to a more meaningful prayer tradition. Our Fathers were prayed on attached beads strung together on a cord while monks said the *Office*.

Even though the laity's prayer life was the main reason behind the creation of a new repetitive prayer form, the change effected the way the early Church approached devotional prayer. People were not just praying around holy wells or tossing pebbles, they were devoutly praying "fifties" of Our Fathers before God in church in union with the religious praying the *Office*. This new repetitive style laid the foundation for the laity's next spiritual step into what became known as the Psalter movement.

When we speak about a Psalter there is only one. It is referred to as the Hebrew Book of Psalms. Found in the Old Testament, the Book of Psalms contains a collection of one hundred fifty songs and prayers. The majority of these were composed for liturgical purposes. However, as time progressed so did the functions of the Psalter. The Psalter provided compiled prayers and songs and featured devotional materials like canticles, which were sacred hymns composed of words taken from a biblical text other than the Book of Psalms. The Song of Solomon is one example. Children and adults learned to read from Psalters because Latin was becoming easier to understand. They used these texts both at home and at church.

In the early 14th Century, the *Liber Niger* (Black Book) was found to contain copies of documents relating to Christ Church Priory, Dublin, Ireland. This was an example of a medieval manuscript used by the monastic community. Another example is the Psalter made for Stephan of Derby, the kneeling supplicant, in East Anglia, England, (AD 1348-1382); it contains a music manuscript intended for the recitation of the Divine Office by the choir.

Following the Reformation (1517-1648), services were no longer held in Latin but English. Henry the VIII (1491-1547) claimed to be head of the Church in England (AD 1534) and Ireland (AD 1536). During his rule English replaced Latin. The Book of Common Prayer was in use by the year AD 1549. A century later, the Book of Common Prayer was outlawed.

Liber Albus (the White Book) was compiled by Thomas Fich (died AD 1518) and contains more copies of documents related to Christ Church Priory. Manuscripts from the Medieval Period (from the 5th century to the 15th century)—starting with the Book of Obis, a 15th Century register of leading figures in Christ Church—exhort the community to pray for them. These manuscripts also contain a martyrology plus a copy of the Rule of St. Augustine (AD 400). The martyrology is a 13th century register of saints and martyrs. The rule of St. Augustine was required reading by the regulations of the Order on a weekly basis in the Priory. These diverse examples from Christ Church reveal different functions of the Psalters.

When referring to the Church's Psalter movement, we are talking about a time when religious and laity "wrote their own Psalters" and cultivated their own style of devotional spirituality based on their needs.

Oftentimes these were speculative insights into the lives of Jesus and Mary. There are six Psalter styles worth noting that contributed to repetitive prayer and the Rosary's ultimate formation: the Psalter of 150 Our Fathers (The Psalter of 150 Our Fathers in the 13th century included 50 Hail Marys); The Psalter of 150 Hail Marys; The Psalter of the 150 Affirmations of Faith in Christ; The Psalter of 150 Praises of Mary; The Psalter of the Rosary's 15 Mysteries; and finally the Psalter of Rosary Tablets for meditations.

The Psalters

The Psalter of 150 Our Fathers

The Irish were among the first to create a unique repetitive prayer style to help the laity keep pace with them while they prayed the *Office*. This was simply based on the laity praying 150 Our Fathers while the monks prayed the *Office*. By the end of one week everyone had finished praying together.

The Psalter of 150 Hail Marys

The Hail Mary (Lk. 1:28, 42)
Hail Mary, full of grace, the Lord is with Thee.
Blessed art thou among women and blessed is the fruit of thy womb, Jesus.
Holy Mary, Mother of God, pray for us sinners; now and at the hour of our death.
Amen.

While the Psalter Movement slowly emerged, the Hail Mary was growing in popularity and spreading quickly through the Church. It fostered so much inspiration that the Church inserted it into two of its devotional practices: the Little Office of Mary (ninth century) and the Saturday Office, which celebrates Mass in honor of Our Lady. The Little Office of Mary was associated with the Votive Masses of Our Lady for Saturday liturgies. Today it is used as a way of living the hours of the day in union with Jesus and Mary. With all this mounting inspiration, the Hail Mary was receiving a broader acceptance in the Church and its authority was elevated to a higher status.

The Hail Mary Is Published

From AD 1119 to 1354 the Hail Mary was published with the Creed and Our Father in official diocesan decrees around Europe: Durham (AD1217), Treves (AD1227), Coventry (AD1237), Le Mans (AD1247), Valencia (AD1255), Norwich (AD1257), Rouen (AD1278), Liege and Exeter (AD1287). This added more credibility to the Hail Mary. The laity prayed the Hail Mary more confidently as a devotional prayer knowing it was approved by the Church. This growing acceptance toward Our Lady and the Hail Mary cultivated a stronger, bolder faith among the Catholics.

By the 13th century, preachers were instructing the laity on the Hail Mary, including Albert the Great (1193-1280), Thomas Aquinas (died AD 1274), Bonaventure (died AD1221) and Berthold of Regensburg (1220-1272), Germany. The divine inspiration of these men, plus thousands of others, helped popularize the status of the Hail Mary all over Europe. The Church elevated it again granting it equal status with the Creed and Our Father. The status of the Hail Mary could ascend no higher.

A spiritual awakening was now to take place in the Church that had little to do with repetitive prayer and the Psalter movement, but it had everything to do with heresy on a major scale. It is important that we look at this period because it underscores the power of Our Lady's intercessory help in combating doctrinal evil through the Church's men of God. I am referring to the Albigensian heresy and its poisonous influence infecting all of Europe's faithful, especially in the south of France, and the role Dominic would shortly play in combating it.

The Albigensian Heresy

Albigensian, so called after the people of Albi in the south of France, was really a revival of Manichaeanism, a religious dualism that teaches the release from matter through asceticism. It taught that there are two gods and two Christs, denied all the sacraments and claimed that the resurrection of our Lord never occurred. It also advocated suicide and taught that the material world was evil. The Church officially condemned this heresy in AD 1179 and AD 1215.

The Albigensian Heretics

It was during those times when the maternal love, protection and spiritual power of the Virgin Mary had never shone forth with such brilliance for the Church as when it was so radically opposed by the violent heresy of the Albigensians. These well educated heretics spread their doctrines across Europe like a contagion of evil, infecting many countries with their doctrine. They advocated for the existence of good gods, evil gods and pure and material spirits while opposing the material wealth of the Church and its sacraments. This stirred up animosity and persecution against the Church. Such doctrinal evil full of errors not only spread through the south of France and other sectors of the Latin world, it inspired people to bear arms and massacre the Faithful. This evil campaign was so successful it created the impression that no one could oppose and successfully defeat it.

Dominic's Life and the Albigensian Heretics

This is when Dominic, (1170—August 6th, 1221) the founder and parent of the Dominican Order (AD1216) came on the scene. Great in the integrity of Church doctrine, in his example of virtue, and his apostolic labors, he proceeded to debate the Albigensian heretics, not by force, but by trusting completely in devotion to our Lady and her holy Rosary.

Dominic was born into a wealthy family in Calaruega, Spain, and named after St. Dominic of Silos (born 1000), the patron saint of the

Benedictine Abbey of Santo Domingo de Silos. In the earliest narrative by Jordan of Saxony (1190-1237), Dominic's parents are not mentioned, but the story goes that before his birth his mother dreamed that a dog leapt from her womb carrying a torch in its mouth, and "seemed to set the earth on fire."

Dominic was educated in the schools of Palencia, Spain, where he devoted six years to the arts and four to theology. In AD 1191, when Spain was desolated by a terrible famine, Dominic was just finishing his theological studies. He gave away his money and sold his clothes, his furniture and even his manuscripts. When his companions expressed astonishment that he should sell his books, Dominic replied: "Would you have me study off these dead skins, when men are dying of hunger?" In AD 1194 Dominic became a canon regular, a clergyman belonging to the staff of a cathedral, in the diocese of Osma, Spain, under the rule of Augustine.

In AD 1203 Dominic accompanied the bishop of Osma, Diego de Acebo, on a diplomatic mission for Alfonso VIII (died AD 1214), king of Castile, in order to secure a bride in Denmark for crown Prince Ferdinand. The mission made its way to Denmark via the south of France.

When Dominic and Diego crossed over the French Pyrenees, they encountered the Albigensian heretics. They found themselves in an atmosphere of heresy. The south of France was filled with strange doctrines, which had become alienated from the Church and had little respect for Dominic, his bishop or their Roman Pontiff. Guided by the Holy Spirit, he clearly perceived that only preachers of a high order, capable of delivering a reasonable argument, could overthrow this heresy. While traveling to Denmark in AD 1204 they learned that Prince Ferdinand's intended bride had died. Diego and Dominic returned by way of Rome, Italy and ended up in Citeaux, France. There Dominic stayed a number of years in the south working among the Albigensians trying to convert them to the Faith.

In AD 1207, Dominic took part in the last large-scale public debate between the Albigensians and Catholics at Pamiers in southwestern France. A year later Dominic encountered the papal legates, who are personal representatives of the Pope. To them he issued his famous rebuke: "It is not by the display of power and pomp, cavalcades of retainers, and richly household palfreys, or by gorgeous apparel, that the heretics win proselytizers—people that induce others to convert to one's own faith—it is by zealous preaching, by apostolic humility, by austerity, by seeming, it is true, but by seeming holiness. Zeal must be met by zeal, humility by humility, false sanctity by real sanctity, preaching falsehood by preaching truth."

Dominic gathered a number of men who remained faithful to the vision of active witness to the Albigensians as well as a way of preaching which combined intellectual rigor with a popular and approachable style. Dominic laid the groundwork for what would become a major tenet of the Dominican Order over time—to find truth no matter where it may be.

In AD 1215, Dominic established himself, with six others, in a house given by Pierre Seila, a rich resident of Toulouse. He subjected himself and his companions to the monastic rules of prayers and penance; meanwhile bishop Foulques gave them written authority to preach throughout the territory of Toulouse. Thus the scheme of establishing an order of preaching friars began to assume definite shape. Dominic dreamed of seven stars enlightening the world, which represented himself and his six friends. The final results of his deliberations was the establishment of his Order. In the same year as the Fourth Lateran Council, Dominic and Foulques went to Rome to secure the approval of Pope Innocent III (AD1160—July 16th, AD1216). Dominic returned to Rome a year later and was finally granted written authority in December 1216 and January 1217 by the new Pope Honorous III (AD 1148—March 18th, AD 1227) for the order to be renamed the Order of Preachers.

When he arrived in Bologna, Italy, in January 1218, he saw immediately that this university city was most convenient as his center of activity. Geginald of Orleans (1180-1220) established a convent at the Mascarella church. Soon afterwards the community had to move the church of San Nicolo of the Vineyards. Dominic settled in his church and held the first two General Chapters of the Order. He died there at the age of fifty-two surrounded by his religious community. Dominic was moved into a simple sarcophagus—a funeral receptacle for a corpse, most commonly cut from stone—in 1233. Later on this church was expanded and grew into the Basilica of St. Dominic, consecrated by Pope Innocent IV (1195—December 7th, 1254) in 1251. On July 13th, 1234, Dominic was canonized by Pope Gregory IX (March 19th, 1227—August 22nd, 1241).

Throughout his life Dominic is said to have zealously practiced rigorous self-denial. He wore a hair shirt and an iron (chains, girdle) around his loins, which he never laid aside, even in sleep. He abstained from meat and observed stated fasts and periods of silence. He selected the worst accommodations and the poorest quality clothes, never allowing himself the luxury of a bed. When traveling, he journeyed with the spiritual instruction and prayers. As soon as he passed a city or village he took off his shoes and however sharp the stones were, walked the course.

Dominic, divinely enlightened, utilized several spiritual gifts and made many worthy contributions to the Church. He truly used the gift of discernment pertaining to the will of God. He perceived that no remedy would be more adapted to the evils of his time than that men should return to Christ by frequent meditation on the salvation he obtained for us. He composed a Rosary to recall the mysteries of our salvation in succession, and the subject of meditation was as it were, interlaced with the Angelic salutation and the prayer addressed to God, the Father of Our Lord Jesus Christ. Dominic was the first to divide the lives of our Lord and our Lady into 15 mysteries of faith which stand for the virtues and actions that must rule our lives throughout the course of our life. He was the first to institute devotion to the Virgin Mary under the name of the Holy Rosary, establishing the Confraternity of the Most Holy Rosary (also known as the Militia of Christ); today it is a worldwide fraternity of people who promise to pray the Rosary daily. Inspired pontiffs enriched this devotion with further privileges from the treasures of the Church following the Confraternity's establishment (1259) and approval by Pope Alexander IV (1185—May 25th, 1261).

Such a man of God was he! Christ's Holy Spirit truly guided him! He knew this Rosary devotion to our Lady would serve Christ and his Church well, as a spiritual, war-like weapon in destroying the impiety of the Albigensian heretics, which ruled throughout the world (mostly Europe) in the XI, XII, XIII centuries.

Over the decades this devotion would root deeply into the faithful hearts and minds of God's people. Its rich messianic spirituality filled them with divine grace and worked like a balm for those faithful wounded by malicious contemporaries. Eventually, the Albigensian heresy subsided, then fell apart altogether. By the end of the thirteenth century heresy of this kind was rooted out from European society for the most part. The Church was restored to union. Those who wandered away from it returned. The forces of wickedness were destroyed and dispersed. Once again, the faith issued forth unharmed and more shining than before. The Virgin proved she is always ready to help the Church and Christian peoples in their necessities and times of need. Such was the life and ministry of St. Dominic in building up the body of Christ while defending the Christian faith.

The Hail Mary is Joined to the Our Father

By AD 1310 the Hail Mary was joined to the Our Father. In the event that anyone wanted to pray it more, it was done in groups of fifty, a hundred or a hundred-fifty according to the Irish *Na tri coicat* format. Various records show the kind of impact this Irish tradition had on the Church. It cut across the ecclesial spectrum capturing the attention and devotional desires of people from all segments of life. Records show rich and poor, saint and sinner, hermit and laity, as well as the politically powerful prayed the Hail Mary for their spiritual needs. The hermit Aybert (1060-1140) said it a hundred-fifty times—the first hundred Hail Marys were said as he genuflected; the last fifty were said as he prostrated himself on the ground before the Lord. Louis IX, King of France, (April 25th, 1214—August 25th, 1270) would pray each evening kneeling down then slowly stand up saying a Hail Mary; he repeated this process fifty times. Lay people, individually and in groups, prayed Hail Marys on a daily basis in honor of Mary.

The Psalters (Continued)

The Psalter of 150 Affirmations of Faith in Christ, The Jesus Psalter

The Psalter of 150 Affirmations of Faith in Christ follow in the tradition of the previous two, the Psalter of 150 Our Fathers and the Psalter of 150 Hail Marys. The Psalter of 150 Affirmations of Faith in Christ was designed to improve the laity's study of the Old Testament Scriptures, especially the Hebrew Psalms. This served to help them understand Christ on a deeper devotional level and hopefully, discover a special insight about him from the Psalms not revealed in the New Testament. The goal of the study was to uncover deeper meaning about Jesus Christ and his Redemption from a prophetic viewpoint not found in the New Testament scriptures.

For example: Luke 1:30-31 would be compared to Genesis 16:11, Judges 13:3 and Isaiah 7:14: The angel went on to say to her: "Do not fear, Mary. You have found favor with God. You shall conceive and bear a child and give him the name Jesus." Besides, the Lord's messenger said to her: "You are now pregnant and shall bear a son; you shall name him Ishmael, for the Lord has heard you, God has answered you." An angel of the Lord appeared to her and said, "though you are barren and have had no children, yet you will conceive and bear a son. Therefore the Lord himself will give you this sign: the virgin shall be with child, and bear a son, and shall name him Immanuel."

Luke 1:32 would be compared to 2 Samuel 7:12, 13: "Great will be his dignity and he will be called Son of the Most High. The Lord God will give him the throne of David his father. He will rule over the house of Jacob forever and his reign will be without end. And when your time comes and you rest with your ancestors, I will raise up your heir after you, sprung from your loins, and I will make his kingdom firm. It is he who shall build a house for my name. And I will make his royal throne firm forever."

The words of Gabriel: Lk. 1:28 would be compared to Ps. 45:11; Lk. 1:42 would be compared to Ps. 88:36-37; Our Lady greets Elizabeth: Lk. 1:47 would be compared to Ps. 103:1)

The above passages serve as examples for this kind of Old Testament study. However, a complete study would span the scope of Jesus' life—starting with his incarnation through to his ascension into heaven—and would seek to unlock hidden meanings not found in the New Testament scriptures.

I find this type of study enlightening, especially with regard to Jesus, from the standpoint of gleaning more spiritual insight into his life and spirituality (or his mother the Virgin Mary for that matter) from a prayerful examination of the psalms. However, I believe this kind of study is to be done on a devotional level, where an accurate interpretation of the psalms does take top priority and the goal of the study leads to a more intimate union with Jesus or Mary. Notable theologians that were part of this devotional tradition of study include Edmond (died 1240), Stephan Langton (died 1228), Abbot Englebert of Admont (died 1331), and Jerome of Mondsee (died 1457).

150 Praises of the Blessed Virgin

The 150 Praises to the Blessed Virgin was similar in style to the Psalter of 150 Affirmations of Faith in Christ. The Psalter of 150 Praises to the Blessed Virgin focused on the Psalms and excluded the rest of the Old Testament. The Psalms were interpreted to emphasize the glory of Mary's earthly qualities as well as her spiritual qualities.

Mary's qualities were recorded in the form of strophes, a rhythmic system composed of two or more lines repeated as a unit, and praises. These were like the anthologies we have today. The words *rosarium* and *anthology* both suggest the same meaning, a collection of something, in this case, a collection of flowers, poems, or songs. These "flowers" of devotion to Mary's qualities were recorded in groups of fifty and called a *rosarium*. The word *rosarium* means rose garden in Latin and comes from the word *rosaries* meaning "of roses", and is derived from *rosa*, meaning "rose" (1547). In this context, a *rosarium* to Our Lady meant a collection of prayers or praises offered to her from one having a devotion to her. In effect this devotion, or *rosarium,* evolved into a collection of praises broken into three groups forming a hundred-fifty praises based on the *"Na tri coicat"* format.

Four Psalters played an instrumental role in the structure and content of the Rosary. The Psalter of 150 Our Fathers placed the Our Father in the final form of the Rosary format. The Psalter of 150 Hail Mary's created a shorter form of prayer having its own form broken into three groups of fifties. The Psalter of 150 Affirmations of Faith in Christ highlighted the work of Jesus in various stages of his life, passion, death, resurrection and ascension into heaven. The purpose was to deepen the devotion to Christ by appreciating his way of being in the world. For example, one stage in our Lord's life is when Joseph and Mary found him in Jerusalem's temple; this would highlight Jesus' obedience to his parents because he returned home with them; with regard to our Lord's passion, his scourging at the pillar would emphasize his courage to suffer for the will of God. Thinking about Jesus' death on the cross would focus our desire to die in the state of grace; while his resurrection highlights his triumphant victory over sin and death for all mankind. The Psalter of 150 Praises to the Blessed Virgin emphasized the virtuous life and works of Mary by probing into the Psalms using a special way of interpreting them to achieve the desired goal.

Our Fathers and Hail Marys were said in the decade format. The lives of Jesus and Mary were being scrutinized in Old Testament Scripture studies. Their spiritual merits and salvific effects were meditated on and fashioned into written reflections by religious and laity. Devotional spirituality evolved in several different directions much of it built on speculation that eventually laid the foundation for the Rosary meditations. Today much of the Church's Marian theology grew from the work done in these earlier centuries.

By the 13th Century the next two Psalter styles synthesized the previous four. The first Psalter version combined the Psalter of Our Fathers with the Psalter of Hail Marys. This synthesis used a series of meditations recited together based on the lives of Jesus and Mary. Monasteries adopted the format. Monks recited forty to fifty Our Fathers and Hail Marys every day as part of their community prayers; in addition, some of the communities adapted the Apostle's Creed.

The second Psalter synthesized the 150 Affirmations of Faith in Christ with the 150 Praises of Mary. This synthesis created a more unique style. It attached the affirmations of Christ to strung beads. Each bead had its own meditation. The religious developed affirmations of faith into major and minor faith mysteries. A major mystery would be, for example, the resurrection of Jesus (Mt. 28:1-10), a minor mystery would be, when the angel of the Lord descended from heaven: "Suddenly there was an earthquake, as the angel of the Lord descended from heaven. He came to the stone, rolled it back, and sat on it" (28:2-3). Two priests providing major contributions with this tradition are Henry of Kalkar and Dominic the Prussian.

Henry of Kalkar

Henry (1328—December 20th, 1408) was a popular Carthusian writer who combined meditations with beads and subdivided Hail Marys into fifteen decades, each separated by one Our Father. This development was quickly popularized all around Europe, mostly in England, Germany, and Switzerland.

Dominic the Prussian

Dominic the Prussian, a Carthusian monk and ascetical writer, was born in Poland in 1382. He was a confrere of Henry of Kalkar. Dominic died at the monastery of St. Alban near Trier in 1461. Between 1410 and 1439 Dominic attached fifty meditations to the prayer beads based on the lives of Our Lord and Our Lady: fourteen treated Our Lord's hidden life; six dealt with his public life; twenty-four focused on his passion and six were done on his resurrection. For the first time prayer was divided into three mysteries of faith: the Joyful, Sorrowful and the Glorious. The mysteries numbered three hundred and spanned the entire length of salvation history. Some showed similarity to those found in other Psalters, the Psalter of Jesus Christ and the Psalter of the Blessed Virgin Mary.

The final form Dominic organized used fifty Hail Mary's broken into decades. Each started with one Our Father and included one main mystery. The other ten Hail Marys had statements or meditations attached to them but these were subordinate to the main mystery. The final form reflected fifty Hail Marys broken into five decades, each headed with an Our Father and one main mystery related to the Christian faith.

This led to another development: three beads were added with a cross attached to them. When people prayed, they started with the Apostle's Creed prayed on the Cross, followed by one Our Father said on a single bead, followed by three Hail Marys, each assigned to one bead and one intention. On the first bead one Hail Mary was prayed for an increase in faith; on the second, one Hail Mary for an increase in hope; and on the third bead, one Hail Mary for an increase in divine love. By the 15th Century the Hail Mary, Our Father and Mysteries of Faith were joined together forming one homogonous prayer.

Greg Firnstahl

The Psalter of the Rosary's 15 Mysteries and The Psalter of the Rosary's 15 Tablets

The Psalter with 15 Mysteries introduced one mystery per Decade. There was a standardization and uniformity to the prayer. Recitation was simplified due to the reduction of mysteries from the normal three hundred.

Today there is evidence in Europe that shows this tradition dating back to the 15th Century. German records have an old altarpiece that has fifteen mysteries dating to 1490, taken from a Dominican Convent in Frankfurt. Spain has a woodcut from the same time period going back to 1488. The Vallicelliana Library in Spain, has a pamphlet from 1561 showing the Rosary's fifteen mysteries.

The last Psalter made a strong impact on how the Rosary was prayed. The prayer was actually not so much prayer as we know it but an artistic picture that expressed love and honor to Our Lady. The laity used these pictures, known as picture prayers, as a form a meditation. In this Psalter there were fifteen pictures to meditate on. The number of pictures affected the number of meditations used by the faithful dropping the total from three hundred to fifteen.

Sometimes I have prayerfully put myself in the presence of God this way, by utilizing pictures of Jesus and Mary to gaze upon, with no prayers formally said. The net effect was peace in the Lord, a sense of calm, a desire for a deeper union with Jesus and Mary.

The tablets were used to teach the laity the main Christian mysteries. They brought prayer and meditation together and served as an evolutionary step contributing to the way the laity prayed. This format for meditation was novel.

Personalities and Doctrine

Alan de Rupe Shapes the Rosary's Structure

The Rosary evolved even more under the inspiration of Alan de Rupe (also known as Alain de la Roche or Blessed Alain de la Roche). Alan was born in Brittany, France on September 8th, 1428. He was credited by many with inventing, popularizing and even revising the Rosary. He began the claim that Saint Dominic was the recipient of it from the Blessed Virgin Mary herself. However, the Jesuit Bollandist Herbert Thurston (1856-1933) and Cardinal Schuster (1880-1954) agree that the first biographers of Dominic did not make this claim. It is clear that Alan began the legend of the origin of the Rosary as a gift from the Blessed Virgin Mary to St. Dominic.

Some experts object to the extravagant miracles Alan relates in his popular book on the subject. Nevertheless, he founded the Confraternity of the Psalter of Jesus and Mary (1468-70) in Doui, France. The first printed manual of the Confraternity of the Rosary, which explained how to say it and laid out the general fifteen mysteries, was published in Cologne in 1476. Alan was extraordinarily devoted to the Virgin Mother and never missed an opportunity to preach about her.

Much of Alan de Rupe's history is speculative because records were destroyed during the wars of the times he lived. He earned his masters in theology in 1474 and professorate at Saint Jacques in Paris, Lille, and Doui, France. His best known work was done in the Rhineland near Cologne, Germany. By the time of his death, he was such a popular figure it is difficult to sift the legend from fact.

Alan helped perfect the Rosary during its final phase. First, he reshaped the way the prayers were said, "giving the greatest importance to the meditative element" which is "the soul of the rosary." Second, he divided salvation history into three sets of fifty—the Joyful, the Sorrowful and the Glorious. Each set was subdivided into five decades which corresponds to our present fifteen decades. Third, he went around popularizing the Rosary, preaching church missions, organizing Rosary confraternities, promoting holy living through prayer, attending mass, and doing works of mercy for the poor and needy.

Alan de Rupe united Rosary organizations and confraternities around Europe into a central office in Rome. He believed the Confraternity ministered to the laity, providing them with more effective Marian formation. He worked to have it officially recognized by Rome. Unfortunately, he did not live to see it happen. His organization got approval the day after his death at Zwolle in Holland on September 8th, 1475. On that day Emperor Frederick III (September 21st, 1415—August 19th,1493) fulfilled his request. A succession of Popes approved Alan's work starting with Sixtus IV (July 21st, 1414—August 12th, 1484). Papal approval for the Confraternities gave them universal Church status. Within two years membership in these organizations had grown to about 500,000 people. By the end of the century they had spread to almost every region of Europe.

There were two requirements the Confraternities imposed on its members: Pray the Rosary once a week and receive Holy Eucharist on the first Saturday of each month. Tradition holds that Our Lady gave instructions to Alan:

It is a very beautiful, profitable prayer, a service which is very pleasing to me, to recite the Angelic Salutation150 times. But more pleasing to me, and much more profitable, is the Angelic Salutation when it is combined with meditation on the life, Passion, and glory of Jesus Christ, for meditation is the soul of this prayer.

Our Lady was responsible for motivating Alan to do this work. She inspired him to the end of his life through apparitions.

Pope Pius V

The Dominican Michael Ghislieri was pope during a time when the devotion to Our Lady and the Rosary became a testament to God's power and grace. He was born January 17th, 1504 at Boscow, Italy, in the dioceses of Tortona. He received the Dominican habit at the age of fourteen in the priory of Voghera. After his ordination he was made lector in theology for sixteen years and for a considerable time was employed as a novice master. In 1556 he was chosen bishop of Nepi and Sutri, and the following year was appointed cardinal and also inquisitor general—the protector of all things traditional pertaining to the Catholic faith.

In December of 1565 Pius IV died and Michael Ghislieri was chosen pope because of his reputation for church reform. Michael chose the name Pius V and in doing so made it clear that he was interested in implementing the spirit of the law and the letter of the law according to the Council of Trent (1545-1563). Pius the V had the Church give solemn recognition to Thomas Aquinus(1225 or 1227—March 7th, 1274) as a doctor of the Church (1567). He had the catechism of the Church completed during his pontificate and made catechetical instruction of the young a top priority for all parish priests. For a long time Pius V cherished the hope of winning queen Elizabeth of England to the Faith. However in 1570 he issued a bull excommunicating her.

Pius V was disappointed in England but there was compensation the following year when the Holy See was aided politically and materially by Don John of Austria (1547-1578) and Marcantonio Colonna, a Duke and Prince of Paliano, Italy (1535—August 1st, 1584). Marcantonio was both a general and admiral; he was later confirmed by Pope Gregory XIII (January 7th, 1502—April 10th, 1585) after the Battle of Lepanto as Captain of the Church.

Pope Pius V and the Battle of Lepanto

The Power of the Rosary Prayer
October 7th, 1571

On October 7th around 8:00 a.m. a naval battle broke out between Christian naval forces and the Ottomans in the strait between the gulfs of Patrai and Corinth, off Lepanto (*Navpaktos*) that lasted about eight hours. The victory went to the Christian Holy League naval forces under the command of Don John of Austria (February 24th, 1547—October 1st, 1578). Thus bringing to an end the final major naval battle fought between rowing vessels. No longer would the myth that the Ottoman naval power was invincible be held in belief.

The forces included a Holy alliance with the Church and its allies: the Republic of Venice; Spain; the Papal States; the Republic of Genoa; the Duchy of Savoy; and the Knights of Malta. This holy alliance gave the Christians a naval force of two hundred six galleys and six galleasses, large converted merchant galleys carrying substantial artillery. These forces would crush the opposition completely when the time came for battle. This alliance brought to the battle about thirty thousand fighting men, about the same number held by the Ottoman fleet.

The Ottoman fleet consisted of two hundred sixteen galleys and fifty-six galliots. In the Mediterranean, galliots were a type of smaller galley with one or two masts and about twenty oars. Warships of this type carried between two and ten cannons of smaller caliber, 50-150 men, and were under the leadership of Ali Pasha at the time. He died in battle. Prior to the battle various Christian contingencies met the main force in July and August of 1571 at Messina, Sicily, Italy.

The Deployment.

The Christian fleet formed up in four divisions in a North-South line. At the northern end, closest to the coast, was the Left Division of 53 galleys.

The Center Division consisted of 62 galleys under Don John's command. The Right Division to the South consisted of another 53 galleys. Two

Galleasses (fighting galleys) had side-mounted cannons for the purpose of preventing the Turks from sneaking in small boats and sapping, sabotaging or boarding the Christian vessels. A Reserve Division of 38 galleys was stationed behind the main fleet to lend support wherever it was needed. Scouting groups were formed.

The Turkish fleet consisted of 54 galleys and 2 galliots on the right; 61 galleys and galliots in the center; and 63 galleys and 30 galliots in the south offshore. A small reserve of 8 galleys and 22 galliots existed behind the center body. The Ottoman naval commander, Ali Pasha, is supposed to have told his Christian galley slaves: "If I win the battle, I promise you your liberty. If the day is yours, then God has given it to you."

The Battle.

Christ's faithful warriors, prepared to sacrifice their life and blood for the salvation of their faith and their country, proceeded to meet the foe near the Gulf of Corinth. Those who were unable to take part formed a pious band of supplicants, called on Mary; united in prayer they saluted her again and again in the words of the Rosary, imploring her to grant victory to their companions engaged in battle. Our Sovereign Lady did grant her aid; and the Ottomans fell to the Christian fleet. The enemy was routed with great slaughter.

The battle ended around 4 p.m. with the virtual destruction of the Ottoman navy. Around 15,000 Turks were slain and captured; about 10,000 Christian galley slaves were liberated; much treasure was confiscated. The Turkish fleet suffered the loss of about 210 ships—117 galleys, 10 galliots; 3 fustas (or galliots). Casualties were around 25,000-30,000 men; at least 3,500 were captured.

The Aftermath.

The efficacy and power of the Rosary was wonderfully exhibited throughout this naval battle; the Church credited the victory to the Virgin Mary, whose intercession to God they had implored. Because of this powerful example of Our Lady's intercession through the Rosary, the Church concluded the Rosary was a great weapon and aid against present dangers. And to preserve the memory of this great victory thus granted, Pius V instituted a new Catholic feast-day: "Our Lady of Victory" (1571) to commemorate the victory at Lepanto. On May 1st, 1572, Pope Pius V passed away at the age of sixty-eight.

Endorsements Follow

On that day of victory, October 7th, 1571, Pius V declared the Rosary to be made for the day's liturgy. Two years later, in 1573, at the request of the Dominican Order, Pope Gregory XIII changed the title of the feast day to *Feast of the Most Holy Rosary*. In 1716 this feast was assigned to the first Sunday in October by Pope Clement XII (In 1913, Pope Pius X changed the date to October 7th to restore celebration of the liturgy of the Sundays). In 1671, Pope Clement X (July 13th, 1590—July 22nd, 1676) extended the Rosary's observance to the feast of all Spain.

On August 5th, 1761, the feast-day of Our Lady of the Snows, the Turks provoked another battle this time at Peterwardian, Hungary but were defeated by Prince Eugene's Christian forces. In memory of this defeat Pope Clement XI extended the Feast of the Most Holy Rosary from Spain to the whole Church.

Bishops began publishing diocesan directives that circulated around Europe exhorting Catholics to pray the Rosary. Then followed Church missionaries. These men and women went around Europe advocating the Rosary, teaching its merits and how to pray it. This zeal extended beyond the European shores onto other parts of the globe including the Americas, East Indies, Japan and regions of China. Out of such zeal there are saints deserving special recognition for spreading this devotion to Mary, among them are St. Francis Assisi (died 1226), St. Anthony of Padua (died 1231), St. Bonaventure (died 1274), Duns Scotus (died 1308) and Bernardine of Siena (died 1380).

Through the zeal of saints, popes plus thousands of others, the popularity of the Rosary abounded in so many different ways, teachings, songs and doctrines. A flood of inspiration spread all over Europe and to other parts of the world making the Rosary a prayer of universal recognition and devotion while the Church proclaimed its message with untiring zeal. Yet with all the attention the Rosary received, it had not yet reached its final form.

Albert di Castello

Albert di Castello, a Dominican friar, made modifications to the Rosary's final form. He improved the way it was used for meditation by introducing meditation material to each Hail Mary. Di Castello wrote *Rosario Della Gloriosa Vergine* (published 1521). *Rosario Della Gloriosa Vergine* was unique. It advocated the concept of "mystery" based on a revealed doctrine of faith; as you prayed the Rosary and meditated on its mysteries, you would accept the fact that you could never fully grasp them. Such is a mystery! Its scope and meaning extend beyond the reaches of one's intellect. The Church liked this concept and encouraged its people to meditate this way for the purpose of deepening his or her own faith. This advancement proposed by di Castello united the Our Father in front of each decade. Yet it would not be long before this Rosary's spirituality would be tested, its faith tried. Spiritual warfare was looming on the horizon. Could the power of the Rosary defeat heresy again like it did during Dominic's time in the 1200's? What about Jansenism?

Jansenism Heresy and St. DeMontfort

Jansenism was founded by Jansenius (died May 6th, 1638), the Bishop of Ypres, Flanders. It taught predestination, denied a person has a free will, and maintained that people are incapable of doing good on their own. They need divine help. Jansenism also taught that Christ did not die for the whole world but for only a select few privileged souls. These errors were condemned by Pope Urban VIII (1568-1644) in 1642 and by Pope Clement XI in 1705.

But for now, our next saint, Louis DeMontfort, would become a priest and devote much of his ministry to spreading Marian spirituality, and combating Jansenism through the Rosary, especially in the south of France. Though he did not openly oppose Jansenism in debates like Dominic did, he would counter its teachings and effects primarily through his parish mission work among the faithful.

DeMontfort and the Jansenists

Louis-Marie Gringion de Montfort was born January 31st, 1673 at Montfort, France. He grew up as a child wanting to serve God. On his days off from school he would do volunteer work at the local hospital. Later on, in his mid teens he entered religious life and eventually became an ordained priest by his mid-twenties. After serving in a parish, he entered monastic life and eventually was elected abbot. After serving as an abbot, he left monastic life and did mission work on the Rosary and Marian spirituality around the South of France.

It is well known that DeMontfort served an important role in the history of the Rosary. He traveled around France conducting missions and stood on street corners initiating conversations with the locals, praying with them and talking about Our Lady. He started self-support groups (Wisdom Groups) for the edification of local parishioners. What he wanted to do was make Our Lady accessible to all who would listen and desire to follow her. He worked "ardently and efficaciously" toward that goal. DeMontfort also wrote several books, in particular, *The Secret of the Rosary.* (You can buy a copy at your local Catholic bookstore or online.) *The Secret of the Rosary* inspires people to pray the Rosary and trust our Lady's intercession. It retells numerous stories about the Rosary's powerful effects on the lives of those who pray it. In fact, it is so well written, Pope John Paul II (May 18th, 1920—April 2nd, 2005) refers to it in his world-class encyclical, *Rosarium Virginis Maraie,* as an "excellent work, "while the Church regards it as a spiritual classic. On April 28th, 1716, this great herald of the gospel passed away. In 1888 Pope Leo XIII (March 2nd, 1810—July 20th, 1903) beatified him and in 1947 Pius XII (1876-1958) canonized him St. Louis-Marie Gringion DeMontfort.

Assumption of the Blessed Virgin Mary

"Munificentissimus"

On November 1st, 1950, a truth of the Catholic faith was proclaimed as a dogma by Pope Pius XII, which holds that "the Immaculate Mother of God, Mary ever-Virgin Mary, when the course of her earthly life was finished, was taken up body and soul into the glory of heaven . . . and exalted by the Lord as Queen over all things so that she might be the more fully conformed to her son, the Lord of lords and the conqueror of sin and death" (*Catechism of the Catholic Church,* # 966). This belief was evident from the very earliest days of the Church. The feast of Mary's Assumption, celebrated on August 15, is one of the principal feasts of the Church year and is for Roman Catholics a holy day of obligation. It is also one of the Rosary's principal mysteries of faith: the fourth glorious mystery is the Assumption of Mary.

A Pilgrim's History of the Rosary

There is no direct biblical evidence about what happened to the Virgin Mother after the death of her son. It is believed she died here at this site in a house similar to this one. Its foundation dates to the first century, while the house dates to the sixth. The domed structure was renovated in 1950.

Inside is a small-lit chapel lining the sides of the main room. Here Pope Paul VI celebrated Mass in 1967, and in 1979 Pope John Paul visited, proclaiming it a place of worship. Meryemana *is sacred.*

An icon of Mary is displayed in the brick alcove on the altar's right side. In 787 the Roman empress Irene called the Church's seventh ecumenical council at Nicaea to settle the issue about the valid to use icons, and other venerate sacred images in the Church. Iconoclasts opposed this and were condemned by the council.

Outside the house, down a small set of stairs pilgrims may draw water from the holy spring. This water is known to possess healing properties.

The Luminous Mysteries

On October 16th, 2002, Pope John Paul II issued from the Vatican the Apostolic Letter, On The Most Holy Rosary, *"Rosarium Virginis Mariae"*. This apostolic letter attributes the Rosary's evolving form to the Holy Spirit's guidance. Its profound simplicity and its spiritual nature are fertile ground yielding a harvest of holiness in the lives of those who pray it.

Pope John Paul II recognizes his predecessors' contributions to the Rosary and felt inspired to establish the Year of the Rosary, October 2002-October 2003. In this context he offers his own contribution, a reflection on the Rosary and the new Luminous Mysteries of Faith, which exhorts us to start afresh by contemplating the face of Christ in union with, and at the feet of Mary. The most important reason the Pope encourages the faithful to pray the Rosary is it serves as a path of contemplation. It fosters a commitment to contemplation of the Christian mystery as proposed in *Novo Miillennio*

Ineunte (January 6th, 2001) as a genuine "training in Holiness" so our Christian communities become "genuine schools of prayer."

In chapter one, Contemplating Christ With Mary, we are exhorted to look on Christ's face as the Apostles did (Mt. 17:2). This is an opportunity to recognize its mystery for what it is in the daily events of his life—from his suffering to his divine splendor definitively revealed as the Risen Lord seated in glory at the right hand of the Father. To achieve this level of contemplation the Pope exhorts us to turn to Mary as our divine model and be guided by her example as one who faithfully devoted herself to contemplating Christ's face, ever gazing on it and seeking to penetrate its many different levels of meaning.

Chapter Two, Mysteries of Christ—Mysteries of His Mother, calls us to listen attentively in the Spirit to the Father's voice as we contemplate Christ's face. To accomplish this we need a revelation from above and we find this in the person of Christ, the definitive revelation of God and "evidently a mystery of light." Consequently, the Pope looks at the mysteries of faith, the joyful, sorrowful, and the glorious and decides to add another, *the mysteries of light,* which provides us with a "true doorway to the depths of the Heart of Christ, ocean of joy and of light, of suffering and glory."

Chapter Three, "For Me, To Live is Christ," describes the proper method to love and is designed to assist us in assimilating the mysteries of Christ proposed by the Rosary.

In all, the Pope used his Apostolic Letter to introduce us to the mysteries of light, the Luminous Mysteries:

1. Christ's Baptism;
2. His Self-manifestation at Cana;
3. His Proclamation of God's Kingdom;
4. His Transfiguration;
5. His Institution of the Eucharist.

The Pope's intention was to capture the entire depth of the gospel mysteries by adding the Luminous Mysteries, which feature certain turning points in Christ's public ministry. So let us now turn our attention to the Rosary and learn how to pray it.

Introducing
the Rosary Concept

Greg Firnstahl

Praying the Rosary is based on a simple concept structured around certain prayers arranged in a specific order. The introduction is built on the Apostles' Creed, one Our Father and three Hail Marys. Its main body is based on one Our Father, ten Hail Marys, a Glory Be to the Father and the Fatima Prayer; this is called a decade. Each decade has a main mystery attached to it. As we pray a decade, we meditate on one of the mysteries. By praying five decades of the Rosary, we pray each of the mysteries of faith—the Joyful, Luminous, Sorrowful and Glorious. When we have prayed all four mysteries and twenty decades we have completed a full Rosary.

A mystery of faith reveals the grace of God and the presence of God in a life event surrounding Jesus and Mary. When praying, we meditate on a mystery the same way our Lady did and avail ourselves of God's Divine Presence. Praying the Rosary leads us to Jesus through Mary, no matter what the situation is, no matter what the cause. Praying the Rosary leads us to Jesus and Mary. Furthermore it delivers us from evil, either our own or someone else's, or from some sort of situation or problem that can have a negative effect on us; it delivers us and leads us into their peaceful presence.

Praying the Rosary has many benefits. It minimizes sinning in our lives and it increases the virtues of faith, hope and love. It blesses us with the gifts of the Holy Spirit such as wisdom, knowledge, understanding, counsel, fortitude, piety and fear of the Lord. These virtuous graces and spiritual gifts draw us closer to Jesus and Mary. Praying the Rosary bestows peace and joy. Both Jesus and Mary know what we need most, their peace and joy. They know our hearts and our heart's desires. They know what harms us, what helps us, what draws us closer to God, what keeps us separated from Him.

We pray the Rosary with meditation. We don't rush it. It is not an empty mechanical experience with no soul or value; it is not a meaningless ritual that serves no value to our soul or our friendship with Jesus and Mary. We pause and give thought to each mystery as we meditate on it. Realize that the Rosary does not have to be prayed in one sitting, nor that we need to pray a certain number of prayers or decades at one time. But we do need to <u>rest</u> with the Rosary in hand while we open our hearts to God in meditation. As an act of faith, this gives us His divine peace while we are in prayer.

Praying the Rosary allows God to channel His graces in us, filling us in many different ways. As we grow older, we become advanced in the graces of this prayer; its effects take firmer root in our souls with time. We are not the same. We have matured. We have become men and women of God! Our faith, hope and love in God are stronger, more confident. Our spiritual gifts have matured. We have put on the mind of Christ. We behave more like him. We talk more like him. Such is the power of the Rosary—it transforms us.

Praying the Rosary requires persistence. We must try to not lose heart. It is a short prayer, repetitious, a concentrated meditation, and we have to learn to handle the distractions that arise in us while we pray. Praying the Rosary helps us to purify our intentions. When we pray, we are before God; we join our intentions to our prayers to our actions so it inspires us to be more pure in how we pray and how we act.

Pope John XXIII (November 25th, 1881—June 1st, 1963) granted a plenary indulgence to Catholics who offer God their daily labors in prayer using any form they choose, and a partial indulgence of five hundred days when we offer them up with a humble and contrite heart.

The Joyful Mysteries

Pray on Mondays and Sundays from the first Sunday of Advent to Lent.

- ❖ The Annunciation Lk. 1:30-32
- ❖ The Visitation Lk. 1:42-43
- ❖ The Nativity Lk. 2:6-7
- ❖ The Presentation Lk. 2:34-35
- ❖ The Finding of Jesus in the Temple Lk. 2:48

The Luminous Mysteries

Pray on Thursdays.

- ❖ Christ's Baptism in the Jordan Mt. 3:13-17
- ❖ The Wedding at Cana Jn. 2:1-13
- ❖ The Sermon on the Mount Mt. 5-7
- ❖ The Transfiguration Mt. 17:1-8
- ❖ The Institution of the Eucharist Mt. 26:26-30

A Pilgrim's History of the Rosary

The Sorrowful Mysteries

Pray on Tuesdays and Fridays and the Sundays of Lent.

- The Agony in the Garden Mt. 26:39
- The Scourging Mt. 27:26
- The Crowning of Thorns Mt. 27:29
- The Carrying of the Cross Jn. 19:17
- The Crucifixion Lk. 23:46

The Glorious Mysteries

Pray on Wednesdays and Saturdays and the Sundays from Easter until Advent.

- The Resurrection Lk. 24:6
- The Ascension Lk. 24:51
- The Descent of the Holy Spirit Acts 2:1-4
- The Assumption
Pius X, "Munificentissimus"
- The Coronation of Mary,
Pius XII, "Ad Caeli Reainam"

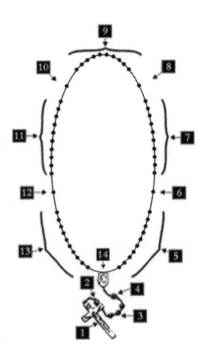

Praying the Rosary

1. Make the **Sign of the Cross** and pray:

   In the name of the Father, the Son and The Holy Spirit.

   Say the **Apostles' Creed** on the Crucifix:

   I believe in God, the Father Almighty, Creator of heaven and earth. And in Jesus Christ His only Son, Our Lord, Who was conceived by the Holy Spirit, born of the Virgin Mary, suffered under Pontius Pilate, was crucified, died and was buried. He descended into hell, the third day He rose again from the dead. He ascended into heaven, and sits at the right hand of God, the Father Almighty, from thence He shall come to judge the living and the dead.
   I believe in the Holy Spirit, the Holy Catholic Church, the communion of saints, the forgiveness of sins, the resurrection of the body and the life everlasting. Amen.

2. On this bead say an **Our Father** in honor of the life God has given you

   Our Father, Who art in heaven, hallowed be Thy name. Thy kingdom come. Thy will be done, on earth as it is in heaven. Give us this day, our daily bread, and forgive us our trespasses, as we forgive those who trespass against us. And lead us not into temptation, but deliver us from evil. Amen.

3. On each of the next three beads, say three **Hail Marys:**

   • The first Hail Mary *for the virtue of faith*—through faith we come to know God and His merciful power to which we appeal.
   • The second Hail Mary *for the virtue of hope*—hope that gives us confident expectation that our prayerful desires will be granted us.

- The third Hail Mary *for the virtue of love*—love that governs our desires, which brings order to our petitions and actions that are pleasing to God.

Hail Mary

Hail, Mary, full of grace; the Lord is with thee: Blessed are you among women, and blessed is the fruit of your womb, Jesus. Holy Mary, Mother of God, pray for us sinners, now and at the hour of our death. Amen.

4. On this bead, announce the **First Mystery**. Think about it for a couple of moments and then pray an Our Father.
5. Say a Hail Mary on each of the next ten beads. End the decade of Hail Marys with a Glory Be to the Father and the Fatima Prayer.

Let us pray:
The Glory Be to the Father

Glory Be to the Father, and to the Son, and to the holy Spirit. As it was in the beginning, is now, and ever shall be, world without end. Amen

Let us pray:
The Fatima Prayer

Oh My Jesus, forgive us our sins, save us from the fires of hell. Lead all souls into heaven; help especially those most in need of your mercy. Amen.

6. Announce the **Second Mystery**. Think about it for a couple of moments, and then pray an Our Father.
7. On the next ten beads, say a Hail Mary on each one and end the decade of Hail Marys with a Glory Be to the Father and the Fatima Prayer.
8. Announce the **Third Mystery**, think about it for a couple of moments, then pray an Our Father.

9. On the next ten beads say a Hail Mary on each one and end the decade of Hail Marys with a Glory Be to the Father and the Fatima Prayer.
10. Announce the **Fourth Mystery**, think about it for a couple of moments, then pray an Our Father.
11. On the next ten beads, say a Hail Mary on each one and end the decade of Hail Marys with a Glory Be to the Father and the Fatima Prayer.
12. Announce the **Fifth Mystery**, think about it for a couple of moments, then say an Our Father.
13. On the next ten beads say a Hail Mary on each one and end the decade of Hail Marys with a Glory Be to the Father and the Fatima Prayer.
14. Let us pray:

The Hail Holy Queen

Hail Holy Queen, Mother of Mercy, our life, our sweetness, and our hope. To thee do we cry, poor banished children of Eve. To thee do we send up our sigh, mourning and weeping in this valley of tears. Turn then, most gracious advocate, thine eyes of mercy toward us; and after this our exile, show unto us the blessed fruit of thy womb, Jesus. O clement! O loving! O sweet Virgin Mary! Pray for us, O Holy Mother of God, That we may be made worthy of the promises of Christ. Amen.

Let us pray:

O God, who, by the life, death and resurrection of Thy only begotten Son, has purchased for us the rewards of eternal salvation, grant we beseech Thee, that meditating on these mysteries of the most holy rosary, we may imitate what they contain and obtain what they promise, through the same Christ our Lord. Amen.

Let us pray:
The Memorare

Remember, O most gracious Virgin Mary that never was it known that anyone who fled to your protection, implored your help, or sought your intercession was left unaided. Inspired with this confidence, we fly to you O Virgin of virgins, our Mother. To you we come; before you we stand, sinful and sorrowful. O Mother of the Word Incarnate, despise not our petitions, but in your mercy, hear and answer us.

Let us pray:

May the Divine Assistance remain always with us, and may the souls of the faithful departed, through the mercy of God, rest in peace. Amen.

On these mysteries of the most holy rosary, may we imitate what they Contain and obtain what they promise through the same Christ our Lord. Amen.

Oh Mother of the Word Incarnate, despise not our petitions, but in your mercy, hear and answer us. Amen.

Praying the Rosary is to embrace strong meditative and contemplative values that focus us on certain virtues and spiritual gifts. These components are rooted in the gospel message. They train us in holiness and empower us with divine abilities. We contemplate Jesus with Mary. We imitate them and conform to their virtues. Both become our all, our shelter, our way to God. We find our peace. Through them God is honored.

Lord Jesus,
Help us to pray the Rosary so you are honored and
glorified through Mary. Amen.

Reflections on the Mysteries of The Rosary

The Joyful Mysteries

The Annunciation

The gospel of Luke has two major annunciation accounts in its first chapter. One announces the birth of John the Baptist (1:5-25), while the other announces the birth of Jesus (1:26-38).

In the first account we find the priest Zacharia serving the Lord in the Temple's sanctuary burning incense. During that hour the angel of the Lord appears to him and announces that his wife Elizabeth will bear him a son in her old age. Great will he be even filled with the holy Spirit from his mother's womb! Zacharia's response: "How shall I know this? For I am an old man and my wife is advanced in years." His words reflect doubt in God's power and plan. Not the response God was looking for so He punishes Zacharia for having such doubt.

While in the second announcement regarding the birth of Jesus, we find the angel of the Lord appearing to Mary and says: "Hail, favored one! The Lord is with you . . . . Behold, you will conceive in your womb and bear a son, you shall name him Jesus. He will be great and called Son of the Most High . . . and of his kingdom there will be no end." Mary wants to know how this can be since she is a virgin? The angel of the Lord assures her: "The holy Spirit will come upon you, and the power of the Most High will overshadow you." Inspired by faith she responds: "Behold, I am the handmaid of the Lord. May it be done to me according to your word."

In these two accounts, Luke sets before us a challenge: Do we believe God has a plan for our lives or do we doubt it?

Are we like Mary who stands in the presence of believing Christians or are we like Zacharia, who doubts God's plan for our lives?

We need to decide where we stand.

The Visitation

Luke's gospel shows Mary visiting her cousin Elizabeth (1:39-56). In this scene Elizabeth, filled with the holy Spirit, praises Mary for her faith. As this is happening, the infant in her womb leaps for joy. "And how does this happen to me, that the mother of my Lord should come to me?" asks Elizabeth.

Can we not ask the same question with regard to ourselves: "And how does this happen to me, that the mother of my Lord should come to me?" Especially in this hour of prayer?

The Nativity

Both Matthew and Luke have nativity scenes regarding Jesus.

In Matthew's gospel, Jesus comes to unite both Jews and Gentiles into God's Kingdom.

While in Luke's, Jesus' birth will effect all mankind, especially the lowly, the outcast, and social misfits, for example. People like these share in the reign of God.

The basic message is this: the infant Jesus is Savior, Messiah and Lord of all people. Because of all this, Jesus saves humanity from sin and alienation from God.

It staggers the mind! The Second person of the Trinity became man, brother, one of us. While at the same time, being completely human, completely divine, possessing one nature. Human life takes on a whole new meaning in Christ Jesus.

What does it mean to you to have Christ Jesus in your daily life?

What about right now? Is Christ Jesus in your life right now? Why or why Not?

The Presentation

According to the law of Moses, every firstborn male child was to be brought to the temple to be dedicated to God on the fortieth day after birth. At that time a sacrifice of thanksgiving was to be offered by his parents. So it was with Joseph and Mary in the gospel of Luke. Both followed this law, even though Mary knew in her heart that the child was the Son of God.

At the same time in Jerusalem there lived a man called Simeon, who was just and devout "and the holy Spirit was upon him (2:25)." Simeon took the child Jesus in his arms and blessed God in prayer(2:29-32). Both Joseph and Mary were amazed at what Simeon had said about the child Jesus. Then he turned to Mary and said: "Behold, this child is destined for the fall and rise of many in Israel, and to be a sign that will be contradicted (and you yourself a sword will pierce) so that the hearts of many may be revealed" (2:33-36).

Anna the prophetess who served God in the Temple by fasting and prayer was also there on the scene with Joseph, Mary and Simeon. "And coming forward at that time, she gave thanks to God and spoke about the child to all who were awaiting the redemption of Jerusalem (2:38)." And when they had performed all things according to the law, they returned to Nazareth (2:38-39)

This story focuses our attention on the faithfulness of God's people. Here Mary and Joseph, along with Simeon and Anna, are depicted as faithful and committed Jews who observe the law of Moses. Simeon is shown as a righteous and devout man committed to God as a priest guided by the holy Spirit; while Anna is seen as a committed women of God serving the Lord in the Temple through prayer and fasting.

How committed are we to serving the Lord and how do we show our commitment lived out in ordinary life? Do we pray and fast enough? Minister to the poor through word and action? Are we guided by the holy Spirit or by our own selfish intentions?

The Finding of Jesus in the Temple

The story in Luke's gospel about finding Jesus in the temple occurs in his youth and is the only canonical story about the young Jesus that is accepted by the church.

As the story goes, each year Jesus' parents go to Jerusalem to participate in the feast of Passover (2:41). Following the celebration, Jesus' parents leave to go home, return to Nazareth, only to discover that he is missing. In fact, he chose to remain behind in Jerusalem so he's not part of the caravan Joseph and Mary are traveling with (2:43-46). Three day pass. Jesus' parents search for him to no avail. Finally they locate him in the Jerusalem temple speaking to the elders and the high priests (2:46). Joseph and Mary, seeing him dialoging with the elders and high priest, approach Jesus and Mary says to him "Son, why have you done this to us (2:48)?" Jesus' reply astounds them, "Why were you looking for me? Did you not know that I must be in my Father's house (2:49)?" Neither Joseph or Mary understood Jesus' reply (2:50). The end result: Jesus returns home with his parents. Mary his mother kept all these things in her heart (2:51).

Let us never take for granted our relationship with God, especially our simple union with Him. We may think we know our Lord, since we have walked with him throughout the course of our daily life for sometime now. Yet it appears to us that He pulls away from us for a season, be it a long or short time. But the reality truly is He has always been there for us. We were in the wrong place. We really didn't know what we were doing during that time. It's like searching for love in all the wrong places. Have you ever done that? Our relationship with God will always be developed in Church no matter what our circumstances dictate at the present time. Let us never take God and our relationship with Him for granted.

The Luminous Mysteries

The Baptism of Jesus

When it comes to the baptism of Jesus the gospel accounts are somewhat controversial in nature. The gospel of Mark shows the baptizer, John, baptizing Jesus. No problem. However, in Matthew's account Jesus is baptized reluctantly (3:13-17); and in Luke's the baptizer is locked up in prison (3:20), so we don't know who baptized Jesus (3:21-22). John's gospel leaves out the baptism account altogether! All we have is the testimony of the baptizer (1:29-34). What all this leads up to is the baptism event that Jesus went through caused a problem near the end of the first century for the early Christian church.

In Mark's gospel account Jesus is not only baptized, His heavenly Father testifies to Jesus' credibility as His "beloved Son" with whom He is well pleased (1:11).

Up to this moment Jesus has been living a religious life with his mother. Now Jesus enters a turning point in his life: he is baptized by John the baptizer and God testifies to the credibility of His Son. Upon that happening, Jesus enters fulltime religious life and ministry with God the Father's blessing.

Sometimes God uses an event to speak to you just as He did with His Son Jesus. Is God using this time in your life to speak to you? Perhaps you are hearing the voice of the Lord at this time. How is the holy Spirit guiding your response? Choose you this day whom you shall serve. Choose the Lord.

The Wedding at Cana

The wedding at Cana in Galilee is the first of seven major signs given by Jesus in the gospel of John, chapter two. It is considered by scholars to be a theophany, where God reveals His presence to mankind through a sacred event. It's a time of fulfillment. This sacred event happens to be a wedding where Jesus, his mother and disciples attend and Jesus ends up turning water into wine. What leads up to this moment is the wine "ran short". At that point Jesus' mother informs her son, "They have no wine" (2:3). Jesus response, "Woman, how does your concern affect me? My hour has not yet come." She turns to the servants and exclaims to them, "Do whatever he tells you" (2:5) Then Jesus instructs the servants to fill six jars full of water and let the head headwaiter taste it (2:8). He tastes what's supposed to be water and discovers its wine. The headwaiter tells the bridegroom about the wine quality and the celebration continues on (2:8-10). Because of this miracle, Jesus' disciples begin to believe in him (2:11). But this in not just any sort of belief in Jesus. It is belief in Jesus as the coming Messiah. The disciple are placing their belief in Jesus as their Messiah and Lord!

Jesus' mother entrusts herself totally to Jesus. When she goes to the servants, she invites them and us to "Do whatever he tells you." What do these words mean to you today? When might Jesus be speaking to you throughout the course of your daily life? There is a lot to think about. Is Jesus Messiah and Lord of your life? In what ways? In what ways is he not? The reign of God is among us.

The Sermon on the Mount

The Sermon on the Mount is about the reign of God on earth here and now according to Jesus (Matt. 5-7). It discloses what sort of person God is interested in, and what kind of person He is looking for to share his rule and life with here and now on earth (5:3-12). In contrast to that Jesus tells us quite clearly what sort of person we are not to be like (5:13-42). Therefore, followers of Jesus' observe his lead: Love enemies. Give alms. Pray properly. Have a right disposition toward earthly matters, this life and coming age (5:43-6:21). We followers of Christ are to be totally dependant on God, who will supply all our needs (6:25-34). Thus we are called by Christ to be God's true disciples by faith, not superficial and phony (7: 21-28).

In the Wedding at Cana, Jesus' mother invited us to "Do whatever" Jesus tells us to do (Jn 2:5). Now Jesus is speaking to us in his Sermon on the Mount. He is challenging us to change our ways for the better, for the sake of the kingdom of God and our salvation. By changing our ways and living a more effective Christian life we enter into and share the reign of God in our lives with others here and now on earth (5:13-16).

Are we following Christ advice? Are we changing our ways? Being more effective Christian witnesses in this world (6:22-23)? Or are we still caught in the trap of being critical about life and others, still judging them (7:1-5)? Let us take a moment and think about what sort of person we are and what sort of person God is calling us to be. Are we listening to Christ's words and acting on them (7:24-27)? What kind of spiritual foundation are we currently building for ourselves (7:24-27)?

The Transfiguration

This story in Matthew's Gospel reveals Jesus taking his apostles Peter, James and John on a hike up a mountainside (17:1). It's during this hike that Jesus is transfigured before their very eyes (17:2). Peter saw it as a good experience and wanted to prolong it (17:4). Yet there's more. While Peter was still speaking to Jesus, a voice could be heard speaking to all three apostles: "This is my beloved Son, with whom I am well pleased, listen to him (17:5)." When the Apostles heard this message they fell to the ground and prostrated themselves before the Lord (17:6). Jesus then exhorts them to rise up and not be afraid (17: 7).

The book of Linsmore states: "Going on pilgrimage without change of heart brings no reward from God." Think about it.

The Institution of the Holy Eucharist

There are four versions of the Lord's Supper (Mk. 14:22-25; Mt. 26:26-29; Lk. 22:14-23; and 1 Cor. 11:23-26).

The mass we attend reflects a combination of all those versions.

The institution of the Holy Eucharist is the high point of our Christian experience. We actually receive the real body and blood of our Lord Jesus Christ into our lives.

Yet how much time do we spend preparing ourselves for this most sacred experience Most people stand around in the narthex area talking aimlessly to one another before mass begins. Shouldn't more time be spent preparing ourselves for this most sacred event? Shouldn't we spend less time talking before mass? What can you do to better prepare yourself for receiving the real body and blood of Christ? How about going to the Eucharistic chapel for some prayer time prior to mass?

The Sorrowful Mysteries

The Agony in the Garden

Jesus' Agony in the Garden appears in three gospel accounts (Mt. 26:36-46; Mk. 14:32-42 and Lk. 22:39-46).

Each gospel account highlights Jesus' suffering differently. Yet I want to focus on our relationship with God. How difficult it can be for us to implement God's will in our lives when we really don't want to! What do we do? This is the reality Jesus is faced with in this difficult, gut wrenching scene.

Our relationship with God is not based on how we feel. It's based on who we are in Christ and how we measure up to doing the will of God in our lives.

What do you think about that?

There is a deeper union with God He calls us to. It's not easy. How can we improve our simple union with God during those trying times? It is emphasized that "change of heart" has more to do with a decision of the will rather than with feelings and emotions. Do you agree?

The Scourging at the Pillar

Only the gospel of John gives an account of Jesus being scourged at the pillar (19:1). This is an event in Jesus' life we have a hard time wrapping our heads around. From a mystical perspective God wants to deepen our relationship with him, so he allows us to be stripped of our worldly ways. Then we are in a place where God can bless us with His deeper union. This at times can be a painful experience for us.

Can you think of any painful experiences you had that brought you closer to the Lord as a result?

In all authentic religions, especially in the Christian faith, a stripping away process of all that is not of God is required of us and is the work of the holy Spirit to do in us. By this process brought about by the holy Spirit we are brought to greater Joy and wholeness in the Lord.

Greg Firnstahl

The Crowning of Thorns

The crowning of thorns in Christ's life is all about public humiliation for him. The Roman soldiers were out to mock and humiliate Christ as best they could. Can you think of a time when God purposefully wanted you humiliated by others and the net effect of it was a closer walk with Him? It's something to think about. No one likes to be humiliated yet this is part of God's plan for Jesus and for us. There are those special times when humiliation purposefully brings us to a closer, more authentic walk with God. During those hard times we need God more than ever. Let us not take for granted our relationship with God during hard times. God is still in control of our lives when times are hard. It happens that He talks to us during those painful moments. Can you think of a difficult time when God spoke to you? Was the outcome of the difficult time beneficial for you? What direction did it point you in? Further away from the Lord or closer to Him?

Carrying the Cross

Through carrying the cross, Christ set before us the example we are to follow when enduring trials. Some trials we just can't escape in life, be they emotional, physical, vocational, for example.

Christian spirituality brings us closer to the those saints who themselves were sinners, weak and wayward. Can you think of any examples? What about St Paul?

Suffering for its own sake can be meaningless and have no redemptive value for some people, but for followers of Christ, suffering takes on meaning and is fruitful when it is associated with Christ's sufferings. Associate your sufferings with Jesus. It may sound trivial but its value is significant and real. Real suffering in Christ is good though hard to take and difficult to endure. It leads us closer to Jesus. What do you think about that? Sounds trivial? Suffering makes us more Christ-like. Being more Christ-like is not a trivial matter. It's what makes a saint a saint. Eventually suffering ends. It doesn't last forever. For the time, pick up your cross and follow Jesus. Pray over it. Follow the leading of the holy Spirit.

The Crucifixion

Every Gospel story has the crucifixion of Jesus. We are all familiar with it. However, we are less familiar with Galatians 2:19-20: "I have been crucified by Christ; yet I live, no longer I, but Christ lives in me; insofar as I now live in the flesh, I live by faith in the Son of God who has loved me and given himself up for me."

Simple union with God for all believers in Christ is all about Christ living in us! Yet so true. To get there requires us to be guided by the holy Spirit to that end because having simple union with God is a gift from God, it's not something we achieve on our own merit. Yet when we experience this simple union with God we can see Christ in other people just like Mother Teresa did, for example, she saw Christ in the dieing person in the streets of Calcutta. Can you think of an example in your own life where you saw Christ in other people? What about the poor? Your parents? Friends? Teachers? Children? Have you seen Christ in the them? Do you have a simple union with God? Pray that God intensify your simple union with Him.

The Glorious Mysteries

The Resurrection

Three days following the death of Jesus a miracle happens that changes the course of human and religious history for all time. The Resurrection occurs. Jesus is raised bodily from the dead by the power of the holy Spirit.

For the Irish, "God's help is nearer than the door"—was an experienced truth rather than a wish.

When Christ is present in our lives then hope is possible. "Welcome be God's holy will."

The Ascension

In other words, you cannot separate the crucifixion of Christ from his Resurrection. They go together. To be crucified with Christ as a believer is to rise with him to new life. Suffering turns into joy. Despair into hope.

In this account Jesus, resurrected from the dead, is seen with his people, ready to ascend into heaven. He gives one last glance around at them, knowing their weaknesses and hardness of hearts he blesses them then ascends into heaven (16:11, 13-14).

The next we hear about the Apostles is "they went forth." Preached. Healed the sick. "While the Lord worked with them."

Is Christ "sending" you forth as his "witness" despite your weaknesses and imperfections? Think about it. Jesus calls you and me to be his witnesses here and now. Imperfections and all. Amazing isn't it? Jesus calls us and at the same time continues to work with us through the guidance of the holy Spirit.

The Decent of the Holy Spirit

The Descent of the holy Spirit is in Acts 2:1-4. Here we ponder Mary the mother of Jesus. In this scene Mary is with Christ's Apostles and disciples patiently waiting on God in prayer. Waiting for the holy Spirit. Didn't she contemplate her son's life from the Annunciation to his death on the Cross to his Resurrection and Ascension into heaven during this time of waiting? At the same time, didn't she feel deeply encouraged over her Son's victory over death?

On the day of Pentecost, didn't Mary's contemplation turn into "a gaze afire with the outpouring of the Spirit (2:2-3)?"

Now Mary speaks to us as she spoke to Jesus' disciples, "urging" us to do whatever he commands. We have the power and authority of the holy Spirit inspiring us to witness for Christ and to live the Christian life. Think about it. How effective is your Christian witness to the world? To those people you work with? To your significant others? What area of your life do you need to improve so you can be a better witness for Christ?

The Assumption of Mary

Christian tradition holds that Mary, along with Saint John, traveled to Ephesus to live out the final years of her life. Upon her death she was taken up into heaven body and soul is a matter of faith the Church holds to. From thence she is in total union with God for everlasting life.

Let us pray:

"O Virgin Mary, that you assist us at the moment of our death when our cold and tremwbling lips pronounce your name with languid voice. May you with your spouse gather those souls who desire naught else but to praise and bless God forever".

Amen.

The Coronation of Mary

From heaven the Virgin Mary "protects us and favors us poor mortals in a very special manner" according to God's will.

"In heaven as Queen at the right hand of her only Son, clothed in golden raiment and all manner of jewels, there is nothing she cannot obtain from Him" for His people.

What do you need from God? Request it with Mary. Think about it. "There is nothing she cannot obtain from Him" as long as it is part of God's will!

Final Thoughts

The history of the Rosary spans about a thousand years, further back if we consider some of its more remote beginnings. Who would have thought that counting prayers and pitching stones would play a part in the evolving development of Catholic devotional prayer? From it, the Our Father, Hail Mary and the Glory Be would be counted. Different methods for praying followed. There appeared to be no logic or set tradition at the beginning. The faithful were praying their own way under no one's real guidance except for the wise direction of the Holy Spirit.

Over time, Scripture studies developed. The Book of Psalms and other Old Testament books were used for devotional studies. People tried to penetrate insightfully into Christian mysteries. They tried to extract meaning from Scripture not found in the New Testament. It was not uncommon for biblical studies to lead to much speculation. This led scholars to develop more meaningful theologies on the lives of Jesus and Mary. Both the laity and religious kept searching for deeper insights. They persisted. Such persistence aided in achieving a more meaningful prayer experience and intimate union with Jesus through Mary His Mother. As the centuries passed, significant contributions for praying the Rosary were made by several people, especially St. Dominic, Blessed Alan de Rupe and Henry of Kalkar. They helped bring the Rosary to its final form. These visionaries had conviction about how it was to be prayed. They took complex formats and meditations and simplified them, gifting us with the way we pray the Rosary today. It wasn't until October of 2002 that the Rosary received its newest addition, the Luminous Mysteries of Faith, by Pope John Paul II. In effect, the Rosary's history has evolved over time in the Church through the guidance of the Holy Spirit. It serves the Church as a devotional prayer that leads to union with God. The Church nurtures this union.

Praying the Rosary is more of an art then anything else. Once we learn the Rosary's proper form, it is just a matter of time before we begin to pray as we feel led by the Spirit. The reality strikes us eventually: that Jesus and Mary are with us throughout the course of our day whether or not we are praying the Rosary. This reality never ceases, says the Lord: "I will never leave you nor forsake you" (see Hebrews 13: 5; Joshua 1:9 and Dt. 31:6). Praying the Rosary makes this point abundantly clear so this devotion is more than a simple prayer. It is a way of entering into union with God through the course of one's daily life. What a way to live in union with God! Having said all this let me conclude by quoting Augustine: "If you think this work of my pen to be in any way useful, thank God; if you find defects of mine in it, forgive them as a dear friend would, granting me pardon and wishing me healing with one and the same heartfelt love."

Recommwding List

Ballintubber Abbey Trust. *Guide Book to Celtic Furrow.*
Ballintubber, County Mayo.

Ballintubber Abbey Trust. *The Rosary Way: Strands of Irish Spirituality.*
Ballintubber, County Mayo.

Bausch, Lawrence D., *The Conversion of the Irish From St. Patrick to 700 AD:* Ekklesia Publications; Carrolton, Texas; 2007.

Boyer, Mark G. *Reflections on the Mysteries of the Rosary.*
Collegeville, Minn.: Liturgical Press, 2005.

Catholic Church. *Catechism of the Catholic Church.*
New York: Double Day, 1995.

De Montfort, St. Louis. *The Secret of the Rosary.*
Translator: Mary Barbour, T.O.P.; Montfort Publications; Bay Shore, N. Y.

Dimond, Bro. Michael. Padre Pio: *A Catholic Priest Who Worked Miracles and Bore the Wounds of Jesus Christ on His Body.* Most Holy Family Monastery; Fillmore, New York; 1-800-275-1126.

Glazer, Michael and Monika K. Hellwig. *The Modern Catholic Encyclopedia.* Collegeville, Minn.: Liturgical Press, 1994.

Gribble, Richard C.S.C. *The History and Devotion of the Rosary.*
Huntington, Indiana: Our Sunday Visitor Books, 1992.

Marcucci, Domenico. *Through The Rosary With Fra Angelico.*
Alba House: New York, 1987.

McCaffrey, Carmel and Eaton, Leo. *In Search of Ancient Ireland.*
Chicago: Ivan R. Dee, Publisher, 2002.

John Paul II. Encyclical Letter, *Dives in Misericordia: Rich in Mercy.*

John Paul II. Apastolic Letter, *Rosarium Virginis Mariae.*

Keller, William. *"The Battle of Lepanto."*
The New Catholic Encyclopedia. New York: Columbia University Press.

Little, Vilma G. *The Sacrifice of Praise.*
Fort Collins, Colorado: Roman Catholic Books, 1957.

Shaw, J.G. *The Story of the Rosary.*
Milwaukee: Bruce Publishing, 1954.

Walsh, John R and Bradley, Thomas. *A History of the Irish Church 400-700 AD.:* Black Rock, Co Dublin: The Columba Press, 2003.

Willam, Francis. *The Rosary Its History and Meaning.*
Translated by Rev. Edwin Kaiser, C.PP.S: New York: Benzinger Brothers, 1952.

Windeatt, Mary Fabyan. *St. Louis DeMontfort, The Story of Our Lady's Saint.:* Rockford, Illinois; Tan Books and Publishers, 1950.

Winston-Allen, Anne. *Stories of the Rose.*
University Park, Pennsylvania: The Pennsylvania State University Press, 1998.

Made in the USA
Monee, IL
17 June 2023